# Spring into Java Development

## Build Modern Backends with Spring Boot, REST APIs, and Microservices

Booker Blunt

Rafael Sanders

Miguel Farmer

Boozman Richard

# How to Scan a Barcode to Get a Repository

1. **Install a QR/Barcode Scanner** – Ensure you have a barcode or QR code scanner app installed on your smartphone or use a built-in scanner in **GitHub, GitLab, or Bitbucket.**

2. **Open the Scanner** – Launch the scanner app and grant necessary camera permissions.

3. **Scan the Barcode** – Align the barcode within the scanning frame. The scanner will automatically detect and process it.

4. **Follow the Link** – The scanned result will display a **URL to the repository.** Tap the link to open it in your web browser or Git client.

5. **Clone the Repository** – Use **Git clone** with the provided URL to download the repository to your local machine.

# Chapter 1: Introduction to Spring Boot

Welcome to your journey into backend development with **Spring Boot,** one of the most widely used frameworks in the Java ecosystem. This chapter will give you a solid foundation and serve as a stepping stone for more advanced topics as you progress through this book. We'll cover everything you need to know to get started: from understanding what Spring Boot is, setting up a project, and diving into its core features, to creating a simple project that you can run and expand upon.

By the end of this chapter, you will have built your very first REST API using Spring Boot, a fundamental skill for modern backend development.

---

## What is Spring Boot? Why is it widely used for Java-based backend development?

### The Evolution of Java Development

Java has long been a staple in the world of software development, especially for backend services. For years, developers have used Java to build everything from enterprise-level applications to large-scale web services. However, one of the major challenges with traditional Java development was the amount of boilerplate code that had to be written just to get a simple web application running.

Spring Framework, developed by Rod Johnson in 2003, aimed to solve this problem by offering a comprehensive and flexible framework for Java development. It addressed the complexity of building enterprise applications by providing features like dependency injection, aspect-oriented programming, and more.

**Enter Spring Boot**

Spring Boot, introduced in 2013, is built on top of the traditional Spring Framework. The primary aim of Spring Boot is to simplify the development of Java applications by drastically reducing the need for configuration. While Spring provided great flexibility and power, it still required a lot of setup and configuration. Spring Boot takes that burden off your shoulders by providing **convention over configuration** and allowing you to focus on writing the application logic rather than dealing with unnecessary setup.

## Spring Boot flow architecture

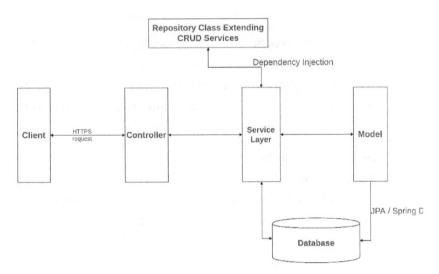

In simpler terms: **Spring Boot lets you build Java applications quickly and with minimal setup.** It eliminates the need for complex XML configuration files, boilerplate code, and unnecessary setup steps. With Spring Boot, you can focus on writing business logic, and the framework handles much of the infrastructure for you.

## Why Use Spring Boot?

1. **Simplicity**: Spring Boot simplifies Java development by providing sensible defaults and pre-configured templates. It also removes the need for excessive configuration files.

2. **Quick Setup**: Setting up a Spring Boot application takes just a few minutes. You can create a full-fledged Spring Boot project with minimal dependencies, and it will run with just a few lines of code.

3. **Microservices Ready**: Spring Boot integrates seamlessly with Spring Cloud, making it easy to build microservices architectures. It provides tools for service discovery, centralized configuration, and resiliency.

4. **Embedded Servers**: With Spring Boot, you don't need to install or configure an external web server (like Tomcat or Jetty). Spring Boot comes with embedded servers, so your application can be run as a stand-alone application with no external setup.

5. **Active Community and Support**: Spring Boot has an extensive, active community. The framework is well-documented and has numerous tutorials, which makes learning and troubleshooting much easier.

# Setting up a Spring Boot Project using Spring Initializr

Spring Boot's ease of use starts with **Spring Initializr**, a web-based tool that lets you generate a project with all the necessary configurations.

## Step-by-Step Setup

1. **Go to Spring Initializr:** Visit https://start.spring.io/, which is the Spring Initializr website.

2. **Choose Project Settings:**

   o **Project:** Choose **Maven Project** or **Gradle Project** (Maven is more common).

   o **Language:** Select **Java**.

   o **Spring Boot version:** Pick the latest stable version.

   o **Group:** Enter a unique identifier for your group, like com.example.

   o **Artifact:** This will be the name of your project. For this example, use hello-world-api.

   o **Name:** This is the name of your application (e.g., HelloWorldApi).

   o **Packaging:** Choose **Jar** (for running a stand-alone application).

   o **Java:** Select the appropriate version based on your development environment (Java 8 or higher is recommended).

3. **Add Dependencies:**

   o For a simple REST API, you only need a few dependencies:

     ▪ **Spring Web:** For creating a REST API.

     ▪ **Spring Boot DevTools:** For hot-reloading during development.

Page 14

- **Spring Data JPA** (optional, for database integration).

4. **Generate the Project**: Once you've selected the dependencies, click on the **Generate** button to download the project as a ZIP file. Extract the ZIP file to a folder on your computer.

5. **Open the Project in an IDE**: Open the project in your favorite Java IDE (such as IntelliJ IDEA, Eclipse, or VS Code).

---

## Understanding the Basic Structure of a Spring Boot Application

Let's take a look at the basic structure of a Spring Boot project that you've just created:

Folder Structure:

Your project should look something like this:

css

```
hello-world-api/
├── src/
│   ├── main/
│   │   ├── java/
│   │   │   └── com/
│   │   │       └── example/
│   │   │           └── helloworldapi/
│   │   │               └── HelloWorldApiApplication.java
```

```
│   │    ├── resources/
│   │   │    ├── application.properties
│   ├── pom.xml
```

**Key Files and Directories:**

- **HelloWorldApiApplication.java**: This is the main class of your application. It contains the main() method and is annotated with @SpringBootApplication, which tells Spring Boot to auto-configure the application based on the classpath.

- **application.properties**: This is where you can configure various properties for your Spring Boot application, such as server ports, logging levels, etc.

- **pom.xml**: This file contains the Maven dependencies required for the project. If you used Gradle, it would be build.gradle.

---

# How Spring Boot Simplifies Java Development Through Convention Over Configuration

One of the biggest reasons developers love Spring Boot is its **"convention over configuration"** philosophy.

## What Does Convention Over Configuration Mean?

In traditional Java development, you often had to manually configure every aspect of your application: database connections, web server settings, and more. Spring Boot eliminates much of this configuration by providing **sensible defaults** for you. Here are some examples:

- **Embedded Server**: Spring Boot automatically configures an embedded web server (e.g., Tomcat) if you're building a web application. You don't need to configure it manually.

- **Auto-Configuration**: Spring Boot attempts to auto-configure your application based on the dependencies you've added. For instance, if you include spring-boot-starter-web, Spring Boot will automatically configure your application to run as a web service with an embedded Tomcat server.

- **Minimal Setup**: You don't need to write configuration files or extensive XML files to get your app up and running. A single annotation (@SpringBootApplication) takes care of most of the boilerplate.

---

# Hands-On Project: Create a Simple "Hello World" REST API Using Spring Boot

Now that we've covered the basics of Spring Boot, let's jump right in and create a simple REST API.

## Step-by-Step Instructions:

1. **Create a Controller Class**: Inside the src/main/java/com/example/helloworldapi directory, create a new class named HelloWorldController.java:

```java
package com.example.helloworldapi;

import org.springframework.web.bind.annotation.GetMapping;
import org.springframework.web.bind.annotation.RestController;
```

```java
@RestController
public class HelloWorldController {

    @GetMapping("/hello")
    public String hello() {
        return "Hello, World!";
    }
}
```

- **Explanation**: The @RestController annotation tells Spring Boot that this class will handle HTTP requests. The @GetMapping("/hello") annotation tells Spring Boot that the hello() method will handle GET requests to the /hello endpoint. The method returns a simple message: "Hello, World!".

2. **Run the Application**: Open the HelloWorldApiApplication.java file, and you should see the following code:

```java
java


package com.example.helloworldapi;


import org.springframework.boot.SpringApplication;
import org.springframework.boot.autoconfigure.SpringBootApplication;


@SpringBootApplication
```

```
public class HelloWorldApiApplication {

    public static void main(String[] args) {
        SpringApplication.run(HelloWorldApiApplication.class, args);
    }
}
```

- **Explanation**: This class contains the main() method that launches your Spring Boot application. The @SpringBootApplication annotation is used to mark it as the main entry point for the application.

3. **Run the Application**: In your IDE, run the HelloWorldApiApplication class. You should see Spring Boot start up and show logs in the console. The application will run on port 8080 by default.

4. **Test the API**: Open a web browser or use an API testing tool like Postman to test your API by navigating to:

```bash
```

```
http://localhost:8080/hello
```

You should see the message "Hello, World!" displayed in your browser.

---

# Conclusion

By now, you've successfully set up your first Spring Boot project, built a simple REST API, and learned how Spring Boot simplifies Java development. In this chapter, you got hands-on experience with

Spring Boot's powerful features, and now you have a solid foundation to build more complex applications.

# Chapter 2: Building Your First REST API with Spring Boot

## Overview

In this chapter, we will introduce you to **RESTful services**, a key feature of **Spring Boot** applications. You'll learn how to build a **REST API** from scratch using **Spring Web**, and understand key concepts like **HTTP methods**, **request mappings**, and how to send and receive **JSON data**. By the end of this chapter, you'll have built your very first **To-Do List API** that supports **CRUD operations** (Create, Read, Update, Delete). This API can be used as a foundation for other projects in the future.

---

### Key Topics Covered

1. **Introduction to REST (Representational State Transfer) and HTTP Methods**

2. **Creating RESTful Endpoints with Spring Web**

3. **Understanding Request Mappings and HTTP Methods like GET, POST, PUT, DELETE**

4. **Sending and Receiving JSON Data with Spring Boot**

5. **Hands-On Project: Build a To-Do List API that Supports CRUD Operations**

---

# 1. Introduction to REST and HTTP Methods

## What is REST?

REST (Representational State Transfer) is an architectural style for designing networked applications. It uses HTTP requests to perform CRUD (Create, Read, Update, Delete) operations on resources. RESTful APIs are widely used in web development because they are simple, lightweight, and easy to integrate into different systems.

Here's a **real-world analogy**: Imagine REST as a restaurant. The **menu** represents the available resources, and you (the client) make **orders** using HTTP methods (GET, POST, PUT, DELETE). The **waiter** (the API) takes your order, performs an action (like fetching data from a database), and returns the **response** (your data or status).

- **Resources**: In REST, everything is a resource. A resource could be a user, a product, or even a task in a To-Do list.

- **Stateless Communication**: REST APIs do not store any session information between requests. Every request is independent.

---

## Understanding HTTP Methods

The most common **HTTP methods** used in REST APIs are:

1. **GET**: Retrieves data from the server. This is a read-only operation.

    o   Example: Retrieving a list of tasks from the To-Do API.

2. **POST**: Sends data to the server to create a new resource.

    o   Example: Adding a new task to the To-Do list.

3. **PUT**: Updates an existing resource with new data.

- o Example: Updating a task in the To-Do list.

4. **DELETE**: Removes a resource from the server.

- o Example: Deleting a task from the To-Do list.

---

# 2. Creating RESTful Endpoints with Spring Web

## Setting Up Your Project

Before diving into the code, let's set up the Spring Boot project. We will use **Spring Initializr** to generate a new Spring Boot application.

1. Go to Spring Initializr and create a new project:

   - o **Project**: Maven Project

   - o **Language**: Java

   - o **Spring Boot Version**: Latest stable version

   - o **Group**: com.example

   - o **Artifact**: todo-api

   - o **Dependencies**: Add **Spring Web** and **Spring Boot DevTools** (for hot-reloading).

2. **Download and Extract** the generated ZIP file.

3. Open the project in your preferred **IDE** (e.g., IntelliJ IDEA, Eclipse, or Visual Studio Code).

## Creating a Simple REST Controller

In Spring Boot, you define **RESTful endpoints** using **Controller classes**. Here's how to create a simple one.

Create a new class named **ToDoController.java** under src/main/java/com/example/todoapi:

```
package com.example.todoapi;

import org.springframework.web.bind.annotation.GetMapping;
import org.springframework.web.bind.annotation.RequestMapping;
import org.springframework.web.bind.annotation.RestController;

@RestController
@RequestMapping("/todos")
public class ToDoController {

    @GetMapping
    public String getAllToDoItems() {
        return "List of all To-Do items will go here";
    }
}
```

- **Explanation:**

  - @RestController: Marks this class as a controller where HTTP requests will be handled. It also returns data directly to the client in the form of JSON.

  - @RequestMapping("/todos"): Specifies the base URL for all endpoints in this controller.

  - @GetMapping: Maps HTTP GET requests to this method. This is where we will return the list of To-Do items.

## Running the Application

To run the application:

1. Open ToDoApiApplication.java.

2. Click on the **Run** button (in your IDE) or use the command line to run the application with:

./mvnw spring-boot:run

Now, if you open a browser or use **Postman**, navigate to http://localhost:8080/todos to see the response "List of all To-Do items will go here".

# 3. Understanding Request Mappings and HTTP Methods like GET, POST, PUT, DELETE

### GET Method

To retrieve a list of To-Do items from the server, you use the **GET** method. Let's simulate a simple list of tasks:

Update the getAllToDoItems() method to return a list of tasks:

```
@GetMapping
public List<String> getAllToDoItems() {
    return Arrays.asList("Buy Groceries", "Walk the Dog", "Complete Homework");
}
```

- **Explanation**: This method will return a list of task names in JSON format when accessed with a GET request to /todos.

## POST Method

Next, let's add the ability to add new To-Do items using the **POST** method. We will accept a new task as part of the request body.

Add a new endpoint in the ToDoController.java class:

```
@PostMapping
public String addToDoItem(@RequestBody String task) {
    // Add the task to the database or an in-memory list (for simplicity)
    return "Task '" + task + "' added!";
}
```

- **Explanation**: @RequestBody is used to extract the task from the request body. When you make a POST request to /todos with a task (e.g., "Buy Milk"), this method will add the task.

## PUT Method

Now, let's allow updating tasks using the **PUT** method:

```
@PutMapping("/{id}")
public String updateToDoItem(@PathVariable int id,
@RequestBody String updatedTask) {
    // Update the task with the given ID
    return "Task with ID " + id + " updated to: " + updatedTask;
}
```

- **Explanation**: @PathVariable extracts the task ID from the URL, and @RequestBody extracts the updated task from the request body.

### DELETE Method

Finally, let's implement the **DELETE** method to remove tasks:

```
@DeleteMapping("/{id}")
public String deleteToDoItem(@PathVariable int id) {
    // Delete the task with the given ID
    return "Task with ID " + id + " has been deleted.";
}
```

- **Explanation**: This method deletes the task corresponding to the provided ID.

---

# 4. Sending and Receiving JSON Data with Spring Boot

Spring Boot makes it easy to send and receive **JSON** data. In fact, **Spring Web** handles this automatically for you. When you use the @RequestBody annotation, Spring Boot serializes and deserializes the JSON data.

### Sending JSON Data in Requests

To send JSON data in a **POST** or **PUT** request, your request body must be a valid JSON object. For example:

```
{
   "task": "Buy Milk"
}
```

In **Postman**, you would:

1. Set the method to **POST** or **PUT**.

2. Set the body type to **raw** and choose **JSON**.

3. Paste the JSON data into the body of the request.

---

# 5. Hands-On Project: Build a To-Do List API that Supports CRUD Operations

## Step-by-Step Instructions

Let's build a complete To-Do List API with **Create**, **Read**, **Update**, and **Delete** operations.

1. **Define the Task Class**: First, create a Task class to represent a To-Do item:

```
public class Task {
    private int id;
    private String description;

    // Getters and setters
}
```

2. **Create In-Memory Database**: For simplicity, we will store the tasks in an in-memory list.

```
import java.util.ArrayList;
import java.util.List;

@Service
public class TaskService {
    private List<Task> tasks = new ArrayList<>();

    // Add methods to perform CRUD operations
```

*}*

### 3. Implement CRUD Methods in the Service Class:

```
public Task createTask(String description) {
    Task task = new Task(tasks.size() + 1, description);
    tasks.add(task);
    return task;
}


public List<Task> getAllTasks() {
    return tasks;
}


public Task getTaskById(int id) {
    return tasks.stream().filter(task -> task.getId() ==
id).findFirst().orElse(null);
}


public Task updateTask(int id, String description) {
    Task task = getTaskById(id);
    if (task != null) {
        task.setDescription(description);
    }
    return task;
}


public boolean deleteTask(int id) {
```

```
Task task = getTaskById(id);
if (task != null) {
    tasks.remove(task);
    return true;
}
return false;
}
```

### 4. Update the Controller to Use the Service:

```
@RestController
@RequestMapping("/todos")
public class ToDoController {
    @Autowired
    private TaskService taskService;

    @PostMapping
    public Task addToDoItem(@RequestBody String description) {
        return taskService.createTask(description);
    }

    @GetMapping
    public List<Task> getAllToDoItems() {
        return taskService.getAllTasks();
    }

    @GetMapping("/{id}")
```

```
public Task getToDoItem(@PathVariable int id) {
    return taskService.getTaskById(id);
}


@PutMapping("/{id}")
public Task updateToDoItem(@PathVariable int id,
@RequestBody String description) {
    return taskService.updateTask(id, description);
}


@DeleteMapping("/{id}")
public String deleteToDoItem(@PathVariable int id) {
    return taskService.deleteTask(id) ? "Deleted" : "Not Found";
}
}
```

## Conclusion

By the end of this chapter, you have successfully built a **To-Do List API** with **Spring Boot**. This simple but practical project covers essential concepts like **RESTful APIs, HTTP methods**, and **JSON data.** You now have a solid foundation to build more complex APIs in the future.

# Chapter 3: Spring Boot and Dependency Injection

## Overview

In this chapter, we'll dive into one of the most powerful features of **Spring Boot: Dependency Injection (DI)**. DI allows you to manage your application's components in a clean, maintainable, and loosely coupled way. You'll learn how **Spring Boot** uses **Inversion of Control (IoC)** to inject beans (objects) into your application, how to apply different types of **DI** (Constructor, Setter, and Field Injection), and how to use key annotations like **@Autowired** and **@Bean**.

By the end of this chapter, you'll be comfortable with **DI** and will be able to create a **simple service** that manages tasks using **DI** in a Spring Boot application.

---

### Key Topics Covered

1. **Introduction to Dependency Injection (DI) and Inversion of Control (IoC)**

2. **How Spring Boot Uses DI to Inject Beans into Your Application**

3. **Types of DI: Constructor Injection, Setter Injection, and Field Injection**

4. **Using @Autowired and @Bean Annotations**

5. **Hands-On Project: Create a Simple Service That Manages Tasks Using DI in Spring Boot**

---

# 1. Introduction to Dependency Injection (DI) and Inversion of Control (IoC)

### What is Dependency Injection (DI)?

**Dependency Injection** (DI) is a design pattern used to achieve **Inversion of Control** (IoC) between classes and their dependencies. In simple terms, DI allows you to inject dependencies into a class rather than having the class create them itself. This makes your code more **flexible, maintainable,** and **testable**.

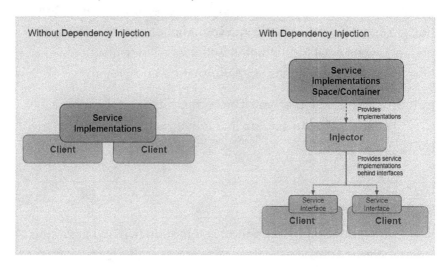

In traditional programming, classes are responsible for creating their own dependencies. For example, if a class needs a database connection, it might create the connection object within the class itself. This can lead to tightly coupled code, making it harder to test, change, or extend. With **DI**, dependencies are provided to the class by an external entity (like the Spring container), leading to **loose coupling** between classes.

### What is Inversion of Control (IoC)?

Inversion of Control is a broader concept where the control of object creation and lifecycle management is inverted. In traditional programming, the class controls when and how its dependencies are created. With IoC, this responsibility is given to an external framework, like **Spring**, which manages the creation and injection of dependencies.

In the case of **Spring Boot**, the Spring **IoC container** is responsible for creating objects and injecting them into classes. This makes it easier to manage the application's lifecycle and dependencies.

# 2. How Spring Boot Uses DI to Inject Beans into Your Application

## The Spring IoC Container

In Spring Boot, the **IoC container** is the core of the DI mechanism. It is responsible for managing the beans (objects) that make up your application. The container can be thought of as a **factory** that creates objects and manages their lifecycle.

1. **Beans in Spring Boot**: A **bean** is any object that is managed by the Spring container. It could be a service, repository, controller, or even a configuration class. Beans are created, configured, and managed by Spring based on the configuration you provide (either through annotations or XML configuration).

2. **Spring Context**: The **ApplicationContext** is the container where beans are stored and managed. The context is initialized when your Spring Boot application starts up, and it holds all the beans that the application will use.

## How DI Works in Spring Boot

In Spring Boot, you declare beans using annotations like **@Component, @Service, @Repository**, or **@Controller**. Once Spring Boot identifies these annotations, it creates the corresponding beans and stores them in the **ApplicationContext**.

1. **Bean Injection**: You inject these beans into other components using the **@Autowired** annotation or through constructor injection.

2. **Example of Bean Declaration and Injection**:

```
import org.springframework.stereotype.Service;


@Service
public class TaskService {
    public void createTask(String task) {
        // Logic to create a task
        System.out.println("Task created: " + task);
    }
}
```

In this example, TaskService is marked as a Spring **bean** using @Service.

To inject this service into a controller or another service, we use **@Autowired**:

```
import org.springframework.beans.factory.annotation.Autowired;
import org.springframework.stereotype.Controller;


@Controller
public class TaskController {
```

```
@Autowired
private TaskService taskService;

public void createNewTask(String taskDescription) {
    taskService.createTask(taskDescription);
}
}
```

In this example, Spring Boot will inject the TaskService bean into the TaskController using **@Autowired**. You don't have to manually instantiate TaskService—Spring takes care of it.

---

# 3. Types of DI: Constructor Injection, Setter Injection, and Field Injection

Spring Boot supports three main types of **Dependency Injection**:

## 1. Constructor Injection

Constructor injection is the preferred and most recommended way of injecting dependencies. With constructor injection, Spring Boot injects the required dependencies into the class through the constructor.

```
@Service
public class TaskService {

    private final TaskRepository taskRepository;

    @Autowired
```

```
public TaskService(TaskRepository taskRepository) {
    this.taskRepository = taskRepository;
}


public void createTask(String taskDescription) {
    taskRepository.save(new Task(taskDescription));
}
}
```

- **Advantages**:
    - Ensures that the dependencies are immutable.
    - Forces dependencies to be passed at the time of instantiation, making it easier to spot missing dependencies.

## 2. Setter Injection

Setter injection is a more flexible approach, where dependencies are injected via setter methods.

```
@Service
public class TaskService {

    private TaskRepository taskRepository;

    @Autowired
    public void setTaskRepository(TaskRepository taskRepository) {
        this.taskRepository = taskRepository;
    }
```

```java
public void createTask(String taskDescription) {
    taskRepository.save(new Task(taskDescription));
  }
}
```

- **Advantages**:
  - Allows setting dependencies after object creation.
  - Useful for optional dependencies, although this is less common in practice.

### 3. Field Injection (Least Preferred)

Field injection is the simplest, but also the least flexible. With field injection, Spring Boot injects dependencies directly into the fields.

```java
@Service
public class TaskService {

  @Autowired
  private TaskRepository taskRepository;

  public void createTask(String taskDescription) {
    taskRepository.save(new Task(taskDescription));
  }
}
```

- **Advantages**:
  - Quick and easy to implement.
- **Disadvantages**:

- o Makes the class harder to test (since dependencies are hidden behind fields).

- o Difficult to see the dependencies at a glance (as compared to constructor injection).

# 4. Using @Autowired and @Bean Annotations

## @Autowired Annotation

The **@Autowired** annotation tells Spring to **inject** the dependency into the class. Spring resolves the dependency and provides an instance of the class.

- **For Constructor Injection**: Use @Autowired on the constructor, but if there's only one constructor, Spring will automatically inject the dependencies without needing the annotation.

```
@Autowired
public TaskService(TaskRepository taskRepository) {
    this.taskRepository = taskRepository;
}
```

- **For Setter Injection**: You can annotate the setter method with @Autowired for the injection.

```
@Autowired
public void setTaskRepository(TaskRepository taskRepository) {
    this.taskRepository = taskRepository;
}
```

## @Bean Annotation

The **@Bean** annotation is used to define beans in a Spring **configuration class**. It tells Spring to create an instance of the object and manage its lifecycle.

```
@Configuration
public class AppConfig {


    @Bean
    public TaskService taskService() {
        return new TaskService(new TaskRepository());
    }
}
```

- **Explanation**: The @Bean annotation is used when you want to define beans manually or when the object cannot be automatically discovered by Spring (e.g., non-annotated classes).

---

# 5. Hands-On Project: Create a Simple Service That Manages Tasks Using DI in Spring Boot

Let's build a simple application where we use **Dependency Injection** to manage tasks.

### Step 1: Set Up the Project

1. **Create a Spring Boot Project**: Follow the steps from **Chapter 1** to set up a new Spring Boot project using Spring Initializr.

- o  Add **Spring Web** and **Spring Boot DevTools** dependencies.

2. **Create the Task Entity:**

```
public class Task {
    private int id;
    private String description;


    // Constructor, getters, setters
}
```

## Step 2: Create the Service Layer

Create a service class that handles business logic for tasks.

```
@Service
public class TaskService {

    private final TaskRepository taskRepository;

    @Autowired
    public TaskService(TaskRepository taskRepository) {
        this.taskRepository = taskRepository;
    }

    public void createTask(String description) {
        Task task = new Task();
        task.setDescription(description);
        taskRepository.save(task);
```

```java
    }

    public List<Task> getAllTasks() {
        return taskRepository.findAll();
    }
}
```

## Step 3: Create the Repository Layer

A simple repository to manage Task objects. For simplicity, we'll use an in-memory list.

```java
@Repository
public class TaskRepository {

    private final List<Task> tasks = new ArrayList<>();

    public void save(Task task) {
        tasks.add(task);
    }

    public List<Task> findAll() {
        return tasks;
    }
}
```

## Step 4: Create the Controller Layer

Create a controller to handle HTTP requests.

```java
@RestController
```

```
@RequestMapping("/tasks")
public class TaskController {

    @Autowired
    private TaskService taskService;

    @PostMapping
    public String createTask(@RequestBody String description) {
        taskService.createTask(description);
        return "Task created!";
    }

    @GetMapping
    public List<Task> getAllTasks() {
        return taskService.getAllTasks();
    }
}
```

## Step 5: Run the Application

Start your application and test the API using **Postman** or a similar tool. You should be able to:

- **POST** /tasks with a task description to create a task.

- **GET** /tasks to view all tasks.

## Conclusion

In this chapter, we covered **Dependency Injection (DI)** and how it works in **Spring Boot**. You learned how Spring Boot uses DI to manage and inject beans into your application, and how to use annotations like **@Autowired** and **@Bean** for different types of dependency injection (Constructor, Setter, and Field Injection). Finally, you built a **task management service** using DI to create and manage tasks.

# Chapter 4: Data Persistence with Spring Data JPA

## Overview

In this chapter, we will explore how to integrate **databases** into your **Spring Boot** applications using **Spring Data JPA**. You'll learn how to set up a database connection, understand how **Object-Relational Mapping (ORM)** works, and map Java objects to **database entities** using **JPA annotations**. You'll also discover how to write **queries** using the **repository pattern**, which allows you to interact with the database in a clean and efficient way.

By the end of this chapter, you'll have extended your **To-Do List API** to persist tasks in a **MySQL** or **PostgreSQL** database, giving you a solid understanding of **data persistence** in Spring Boot applications.

### Key Topics Covered

1. **Setting Up a Database Connection with Spring Boot**

2. **Understanding Spring Data JPA for ORM (Object Relational Mapping)**

3. **Mapping Java Objects to Database Entities with JPA Annotations**

4. **Writing Queries with the Repository Pattern**

5. **Hands-On Project: Extend the To-Do List API to Persist Tasks in a Database (e.g., MySQL or PostgreSQL)**

# 1. Setting Up a Database Connection with Spring Boot

Before we can work with **Spring Data JPA**, we need to establish a **database connection** in our Spring Boot application. This involves configuring **application.properties** to point to our **MySQL** or **PostgreSQL** database and adding the necessary dependencies.

## What You'll Need:

*Database Setup:*

- o Install **MySQL** or **PostgreSQL** on your local machine or use a cloud database service.

- o Create a **new database** (e.g., todo_app for storing tasks).

*Dependencies:*

- o Open your pom.xml (for Maven) or build.gradle (for Gradle) and add the necessary dependencies for **Spring Data JPA** and **your database**. If you're using MySQL, add:

```
<!-- For MySQL -->
<dependency>
    <groupId>org.springframework.boot</groupId>
    <artifactId>spring-boot-starter-data-jpa</artifactId>
</dependency>
<dependency>
    <groupId>mysql</groupId>
    <artifactId>mysql-connector-java</artifactId>
```

```
</dependency>
```

For **PostgreSQL**, you would replace the MySQL dependency with:

```xml
<!-- For PostgreSQL -->
<dependency>
    <groupId>org.springframework.boot</groupId>
    <artifactId>spring-boot-starter-data-jpa</artifactId>
</dependency>
<dependency>
    <groupId>org.postgresql</groupId>
    <artifactId>postgresql</artifactId>
</dependency>
```

### Configure Database Connection

1. Open the application.properties file in your Spring Boot project (under src/main/resources).

2. Add your **database connection settings**. Here's an example configuration for **MySQL**:

```
# MySQL Database Configuration
spring.datasource.url=jdbc:mysql://localhost:3306/todo_app?useSSL=false&serverTimezone=UTC
spring.datasource.username=root
spring.datasource.password=rootpassword
spring.jpa.database-platform=org.hibernate.dialect.MySQL5InnoDBDialect
spring.jpa.hibernate.ddl-auto=update
spring.jpa.show-sql=true
```

For **PostgreSQL**, use:

```
# PostgreSQL Database Configuration
spring.datasource.url=jdbc:postgresql://localhost:5432/todo_app
spring.datasource.username=postgres
spring.datasource.password=postgrespassword
spring.jpa.database-platform=org.hibernate.dialect.PostgreSQL95Dialect
spring.jpa.hibernate.ddl-auto=update
spring.jpa.show-sql=true
```

- **spring.datasource.url**: Specifies the URL of the database server and the database name.

- **spring.jpa.hibernate.ddl-auto**: Automatically manages database schema generation (update creates/updates tables based on entity classes).

- **spring.jpa.show-sql**: Prints the generated SQL statements to the console for debugging.

**Start the Application**

Once your configuration is complete, start your Spring Boot application. Spring Boot will connect to the database and handle entity persistence automatically using **Spring Data JPA**.

---

# 2. Understanding Spring Data JPA for ORM (Object Relational Mapping)

Spring Data JPA simplifies working with **databases** by using **Object-Relational Mapping (ORM)**. ORM is a technique that allows you to map Java objects to relational database tables.

## What is ORM?

**Object-Relational Mapping** is a programming technique that allows developers to interact with a **database** using **Java objects** rather than writing SQL queries directly. ORM frameworks, like **Spring Data JPA**, automatically convert Java objects into database records and vice versa.

- **Java Objects**: Represent entities in the system (e.g., Task class in our To-Do List application).

- **Database Tables**: Store the data that corresponds to Java objects (e.g., tasks table in the database).

## Spring Data JPA

Spring Data JPA is a **Spring module** that facilitates database interaction with JPA (Java Persistence API). It helps with common operations like **CRUD** (Create, Read, Update, Delete) and **pagination**, **sorting**, and more.

Spring Data JPA provides a **Repository pattern**, which is a convenient abstraction layer for interacting with the database.

---

# 3. Mapping Java Objects to Database Entities with JPA Annotations

To persist data, we need to map Java classes to **database tables** using **JPA annotations**.

## JPA Annotations

Here are the key **JPA annotations**:

- **@Entity**: Marks a class as an **entity** that can be mapped to a database table.

- **@Table**: Specifies the table name if it differs from the class name.

- **@Id**: Marks a field as the primary key of the entity.

- **@GeneratedValue**: Automatically generates values for the primary key.

- **@Column**: Maps a field to a column in the database (optional if the field name matches the column name).

## Creating a Task Entity

Let's map the Task class to a database table:

```java
import javax.persistence.*;

@Entity
@Table(name = "tasks")
public class Task {

    @Id
    @GeneratedValue(strategy = GenerationType.IDENTITY)
    private Long id;

    @Column(name = "description", nullable = false)
    private String description;

    // Constructor, getters, setters, and toString() methods
}
```

- **@Entity:** This class is a JPA entity.

- **@Table(name = "tasks"):** The entity is mapped to the tasks table.

- **@Id:** The id field is the primary key of the entity.

- **@GeneratedValue:** Automatically generates the id for new tasks.

- **@Column(name = "description"):** The description field maps to the description column in the database.

---

# 4. Writing Queries with the Repository Pattern

### What is the Repository Pattern?

The **Repository Pattern** abstracts the data access layer and provides a clean API for interacting with the database. **Spring Data JPA** makes use of **repositories** to handle data persistence.

1. **Create a Repository Interface:** In Spring Data JPA, you don't need to write SQL queries manually. Instead, you create a repository interface that extends JpaRepository. The repository provides a set of CRUD methods like save(), findAll(), findById(), etc.

```
import org.springframework.data.jpa.repository.JpaRepository;

public interface TaskRepository extends JpaRepository<Task, Long> {
    // You can define custom queries here if needed
}
```

- **JpaRepository**: Extending JpaRepository gives you all the methods for managing Task entities (e.g., save(), findAll(), findById(), etc.).

- **Custom Queries**: You can add custom methods by simply declaring them in the repository interface, like:

List<Task> findByDescription(String description);

Spring Data JPA will automatically implement this method for you, allowing you to query the database by task description.

---

# 5. Hands-On Project: Extend the To-Do List API to Persist Tasks in a Database

Now, let's extend the **To-Do List API** to persist tasks in a **MySQL** or **PostgreSQL** database.

### Step 1: Create the Entity Class

First, create the Task entity class as we did earlier, using **JPA annotations** to map it to the database.

### Step 2: Create the Repository Interface

Create the TaskRepository interface to manage the Task entities.

```
import org.springframework.data.jpa.repository.JpaRepository;


public interface TaskRepository extends JpaRepository<Task, Long> {

    List<Task> findByDescription(String description);
}
```

## Step 3: Update the Service Layer

Update the TaskService class to use the TaskRepository for database operations.

```
@Service
public class TaskService {

    private final TaskRepository taskRepository;

    @Autowired
    public TaskService(TaskRepository taskRepository) {
        this.taskRepository = taskRepository;
    }

    public Task createTask(String description) {
        Task task = new Task();
        task.setDescription(description);
        return taskRepository.save(task);
    }

    public List<Task> getAllTasks() {
        return taskRepository.findAll();
    }
}
```

## Step 4: Update the Controller Layer

Update the TaskController to handle the **POST** and **GET** requests for creating and retrieving tasks.

```
@RestController
@RequestMapping("/tasks")
public class TaskController {

    private final TaskService taskService;

    @Autowired
    public TaskController(TaskService taskService) {
        this.taskService = taskService;
    }

    @PostMapping
    public Task createTask(@RequestBody String description) {
        return taskService.createTask(description);
    }

    @GetMapping
    public List<Task> getAllTasks() {
        return taskService.getAllTasks();
    }
}
```

## Step 5: Test the Application

1. Start your Spring Boot application.

2. Use **Postman** or **cURL** to send a **POST** request to /tasks to create a new task.

3. Use a **GET** request to /tasks to fetch the list of all tasks stored in the database.

---

## Conclusion

In this chapter, you learned how to integrate **Spring Data JPA** into your Spring Boot application for **data persistence**. You explored how to set up a **database connection**, map Java objects to **database entities** using **JPA annotations**, and how to write queries using the **repository pattern**.

You also created a **To-Do List API** that persists tasks in a database, which lays the foundation for building more complex applications. With this knowledge, you're now equipped to handle **data persistence** in your Spring Boot projects and extend them with more sophisticated features.

# Chapter 5: Error Handling and Validation

## Overview

Every application needs proper **error handling** and **data validation** to ensure it behaves robustly in real-world scenarios. In this chapter, we'll focus on how to handle exceptions properly in **Spring Boot** using the @ExceptionHandler annotation, and how to validate incoming data to ensure that the application works smoothly.

You'll learn how to catch errors effectively and return meaningful error responses to the client, as well as how to use the **@Valid annotation** to validate input, ensuring the application's integrity. Furthermore, we will dive into **custom exception handling** to customize your error responses.

By the end of this chapter, you'll be able to implement custom validation in your **To-Do List API** (for example, ensuring that task descriptions aren't empty) and implement meaningful error handling to make your API more user-friendly.

---

## Key Topics Covered

1. **Exception Handling in Spring Boot using @ExceptionHandler**

2. **Using Spring Boot's @Valid Annotation to Validate Input**

3. **Custom Exception Handling and Returning Meaningful Error Responses**

4. **Hands-On Project: Implement Custom Validation for the To-Do List API (e.g., Task Descriptions Should Not Be Empty)**

---

# 1. Exception Handling in Spring Boot Using @ExceptionHandler

Handling exceptions gracefully is crucial in any web application. Without proper exception handling, users can face vague errors that don't help them understand what went wrong. **Spring Boot** makes exception handling easy, allowing us to define how different exceptions should be handled globally or within specific controllers.

## What Is Exception Handling?

**Exception handling** is a mechanism for handling unexpected situations (errors) that may occur during the execution of an application. In a web application, exceptions may occur due to bad user input, database failures, network issues, or missing resources.

For example, if a user tries to retrieve a non-existent task, your application could throw a TaskNotFoundException. You need a structured way to handle this exception and inform the user with a clear message.

### Using @ExceptionHandler for Controller-Specific Handling

Spring Boot allows you to define methods in your controllers to handle specific exceptions using the @ExceptionHandler annotation.

```
@RestController
public class TaskController {
```

```
@Autowired
private TaskService taskService;

@GetMapping("/tasks/{id}")
public ResponseEntity<Task> getTaskById(@PathVariable Long
id) {
    Task task = taskService.getTaskById(id);
    if (task == null) {
        throw new TaskNotFoundException("Task with id " + id + "
not found.");
    }
    return ResponseEntity.ok(task);
}


@ExceptionHandler(TaskNotFoundException.class)
public ResponseEntity<String>
handleTaskNotFound(TaskNotFoundException e) {
    return
ResponseEntity.status(HttpStatus.NOT_FOUND).body(e.getMessa
ge());
    }
}
```

- **@ExceptionHandler:** The method handleTaskNotFound()
  catches the TaskNotFoundException and returns a **404 Not
  Found** response with a meaningful error message.

## Global Exception Handling with @ControllerAdvice

If you want to handle exceptions globally (across all controllers), Spring Boot provides the @ControllerAdvice annotation. This allows you to write global exception handlers that apply to all controllers.

```
@ControllerAdvice
public class GlobalExceptionHandler {

    @ExceptionHandler(TaskNotFoundException.class)
    public ResponseEntity<String>
handleTaskNotFound(TaskNotFoundException e) {
        return
ResponseEntity.status(HttpStatus.NOT_FOUND).body(e.getMessage());
    }

    @ExceptionHandler(Exception.class)
    public ResponseEntity<String>
handleGenericException(Exception e) {
        return
ResponseEntity.status(HttpStatus.INTERNAL_SERVER_ERROR)
.body("An unexpected error occurred.");
    }
}
```

- **@ControllerAdvice**: This annotation allows you to define global exception handlers. The handleGenericException() method catches all exceptions (not just TaskNotFoundException) and returns a **500 Internal Server Error** with a generic error message.

# 2. Using Spring Boot's @Valid Annotation to Validate Input

In any application, validating incoming data is essential to ensure the correctness of the information before performing any business logic. Spring Boot provides **@Valid** annotation to make it easy to validate input data in your controllers and services.

## Why Validate Input?

Data validation helps ensure that the data entered by users meets your expectations and prevents invalid or malicious data from entering your system. For example, in a task management application, it is critical that a task description is not empty before the task is saved to the database.

### Using @Valid to Validate Input

The @Valid annotation is used in Spring Boot to trigger validation on incoming request bodies, such as @RequestBody data or form inputs.

```
import javax.validation.constraints.NotBlank;


public class Task {
    private Long id;


    @NotBlank(message = "Description must not be empty")
    private String description;


    // Getters and Setters
```

*}*

- **@NotBlank**: The @NotBlank annotation is part of the **Java Validation API** and ensures that the task description is not empty or null. The message attribute provides a custom error message when validation fails.

## Validating Input in Controllers

Once you've annotated your data model with validation annotations like @NotBlank, you can use the @Valid annotation in the controller to trigger the validation.

```
import org.springframework.web.bind.annotation. *;

import javax.validation.Valid;

@RestController
@RequestMapping("/tasks")
public class TaskController {

    @PostMapping
    public ResponseEntity<String> createTask(@Valid
@RequestBody Task task) {
        // Logic to create the task

        return
ResponseEntity.status(HttpStatus.CREATED).body("Task
created!");
    }
}
```

- **@Valid**: This triggers the validation of the Task object before it's passed into the method. If the task's description is empty, the request will automatically return a validation error response.

## Handling Validation Errors

When validation fails, Spring Boot automatically returns a **400 Bad Request** response with a message indicating which field failed validation. You can customize this behavior by using **@ExceptionHandler**.

```
@ControllerAdvice
public class GlobalExceptionHandler {

    @ExceptionHandler(MethodArgumentNotValidException.class)
    public ResponseEntity<String>
handleValidationExceptions(MethodArgumentNotValidException
e) {
        String errorMessage =
e.getBindingResult().getAllErrors().stream()
                .map(ObjectError::getDefaultMessage)
                .collect(Collectors.joining(", "));
        return
ResponseEntity.status(HttpStatus.BAD_REQUEST).body(errorMessage);
    }
}
```

- **MethodArgumentNotValidException**: This exception is thrown when validation fails. The handleValidationExceptions() method extracts the error messages and returns them in the response.

# 3. Custom Exception Handling and Returning Meaningful Error Responses

When building real-world applications, you often need to define custom exceptions to handle specific error scenarios. Spring Boot allows you to create **custom exception classes** and handle them effectively.

## Creating a Custom Exception

Let's define a TaskNotFoundException that will be thrown when a task is not found in the database.

```
public class TaskNotFoundException extends RuntimeException {

    public TaskNotFoundException(String message) {
        super(message);
    }
}
```

- **Custom Exception**: The TaskNotFoundException class extends RuntimeException and provides a constructor to pass in an error message.

## Customizing Error Responses

You can customize the error response format by creating a **global exception handler** using **@ControllerAdvice** and returning a structured response.

```
public class ErrorResponse {
    private int status;
    private String message;
```

```java
private String timestamp;

// Constructor, Getters, Setters
}


@ControllerAdvice
public class GlobalExceptionHandler {

    @ExceptionHandler(TaskNotFoundException.class)
    public ResponseEntity<ErrorResponse>
handleTaskNotFound(TaskNotFoundException e) {
        ErrorResponse errorResponse = new ErrorResponse(
        HttpStatus.NOT_FOUND.value(),
        e.getMessage(),
        LocalDateTime.now().toString()
        );
        return new ResponseEntity<>(errorResponse,
HttpStatus.NOT_FOUND);
    }
}
```

- **ErrorResponse**: This class contains the structure for error responses, including the status, message, and timestamp.

- **Customizing the Response**: In the handleTaskNotFound() method, we return an **ErrorResponse** with detailed information about the error.

# 4. Hands-On Project: Implement Custom Validation for the To-Do List API (e.g., Task Descriptions Should Not Be Empty)

Now that you understand error handling and validation, let's implement a **custom validation** for the **To-Do List API**.

### Step 1: Task Entity Validation

First, add the @NotBlank annotation to the Task entity to ensure that the task description is not empty.

```
import javax.validation.constraints.NotBlank;

public class Task {
    private Long id;

    @NotBlank(message = "Description must not be empty")
    private String description;

    // Getters and Setters
}
```

### Step 2: Create the Validation Logic in Controller

Next, we'll use the @Valid annotation in the TaskController to validate the incoming request body.

```
@RestController
@RequestMapping("/tasks")
public class TaskController {
```

```
@PostMapping

public ResponseEntity<String> createTask(@Valid
@RequestBody Task task) {

    // Logic to create the task

    return
ResponseEntity.status(HttpStatus.CREATED).body("Task
created!");

    }

}
```

This ensures that the **task description** must not be empty when creating a task.

---

## Step 3: Global Validation Error Handling

We'll add **global error handling** to return meaningful error messages when validation fails.

```
@ControllerAdvice

public class GlobalExceptionHandler {


    @ExceptionHandler(MethodArgumentNotValidException.class)

    public ResponseEntity<String>
handleValidationExceptions(MethodArgumentNotValidException
e) {

        String errorMessage =
e.getBindingResult().getAllErrors().stream()

                .map(ObjectError::getDefaultMessage)

                .collect(Collectors.joining(", "));
```

```
    return
ResponseEntity.status(HttpStatus.BAD_REQUEST).body(errorMe
ssage);
    }
}
```

## Conclusion

In this chapter, we learned how to **handle exceptions** and **validate input** in a Spring Boot application. We explored Spring Boot's **@ExceptionHandler** and **@Valid** annotations for validating and handling errors. We also saw how to create custom exceptions and return meaningful error responses to the client.

By implementing custom validation and error handling in our **To-Do List API**, we made it more robust and user-friendly. This ensures that users get clear feedback when they make a mistake and that the application behaves reliably in different scenarios.

# Chapter 6: Securing Your Spring Boot Application with JWT Authentication

## Overview

Security is a critical component of any modern web application. Securing your **Spring Boot APIs** is essential, especially when dealing with sensitive user data and interactions. In this chapter, we'll focus on **JWT (JSON Web Token)** authentication, a widely-used and powerful way to secure your RESTful APIs.

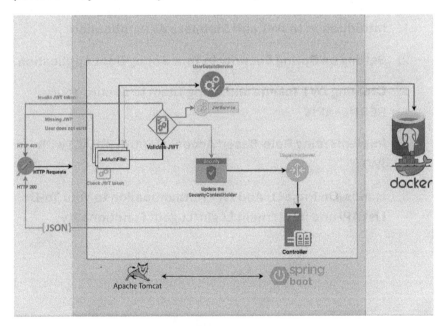

You'll learn how to:

- Understand the basics of **JWT** and how it is used for stateless authentication.

- Set up **Spring Security** in your Spring Boot application.

- Create **JWT tokens** and use them to secure your API endpoints.

- Implement **role-based access control (RBAC)** with JWT for more granular control over who can access certain resources.

By the end of this chapter, you'll have successfully added **JWT authentication** to your **To-Do List API**, implementing both **login** and **logout** functionality.

## Key Topics Covered

1. **Introduction to JWT and Stateless Authentication**

2. **Setting up Spring Security in Your Spring Boot Application**

3. **Creating JWT Tokens and Using Them to Secure Your RESTful APIs**

4. **Implementing Role-Based Access Control (RBAC) with JWT**

5. **Hands-On Project: Add JWT Authentication to Your To-Do List API and Implement Login/Logout Functionality**

# 1. Introduction to JWT and Stateless Authentication

## What is JWT?

**JWT (JSON Web Token)** is an open standard for securely transmitting information between parties as a JSON object. It is compact, URL-safe, and can be used for authentication and information exchange.

JWT is **stateless**, meaning that once a user logs in and is authenticated, the token contains all the necessary information to authorize the user. The server doesn't need to keep track of sessions, making JWT a perfect fit for scalable, modern web applications.

### JWT Structure

A **JWT** consists of three parts, each separated by a dot (.):

1. **Header**: Contains metadata about the token, including the algorithm used for signing (usually HMAC SHA256 or RSA).

2. **Payload**: Contains the claims (data), such as user information or any other data you want to include (e.g., user role, expiration time).

3. **Signature**: The signature ensures that the token has not been altered. It is created by combining the header, payload, and a secret key, and then signing it using the specified algorithm.

Here's an example of a JWT:

eyJhbGciOiJIUzI1NiIsInR5cCI6IkpXVCJ9.eyJzdWIiOiIxMjM0NTY3ODk wIiwibmFtZSI6IkpvaG4gRG9lIiwiaWF0IjoxNTE2MjM5MDIyfQ.SflKxwR JSMeKKF2QT4fwpMeJf36POk6yJV_adQssw5c

## Stateless Authentication

In a **stateless** authentication system, each request sent to the server includes all the information needed to authenticate and authorize the user. Unlike traditional session-based authentication, where the server maintains session data, with **JWT**, the server does not store any session information.

Once a JWT is issued to a user, it can be used to authenticate future requests by including it in the HTTP header (usually Authorization: Bearer <token>).

# 2. Setting up Spring Security in Your Spring Boot Application

Before implementing JWT authentication, you need to set up **Spring Security** in your Spring Boot application. Spring Security is a powerful and customizable authentication and access control framework.

## Adding Spring Security Dependencies

In your **pom.xml** (for Maven), you need to add the Spring Security dependency:

```
<dependency>
    <groupId>org.springframework.boot</groupId>
    <artifactId>spring-boot-starter-security</artifactId>
</dependency>
```

For *Gradle*, add this to your *build.gradle*:

```
implementation 'org.springframework.boot:spring-boot-starter-security'
```

## Basic Security Configuration

Spring Security provides **basic authentication** by default. For custom configurations (like JWT), we need to extend and customize the default security configuration.

Create a class to customize the security configuration:

```java
import org.springframework.context.annotation.Bean;

import org.springframework.context.annotation.Configuration;

import org.springframework.security.config.annotation.web.builders.HttpSecurity;

import org.springframework.security.config.annotation.web.configuration.EnableWebSecurity;

import org.springframework.security.config.annotation.web.configuration.WebSecurityConfigurerAdapter;


@Configuration
@EnableWebSecurity
public class SecurityConfig extends WebSecurityConfigurerAdapter {


    @Override
    protected void configure(HttpSecurity http) throws Exception {
        http.csrf().disable()
        .authorizeRequests()
        .antMatchers("/auth/**").permitAll()  // Permit all for login and register endpoints
```

*.anyRequest().authenticated();  // All other requests must be authenticated*

*}*

*}*

This configuration disables **CSRF** (Cross-Site Request Forgery) protection (which is not needed for APIs) and requires authentication for all endpoints except those under /auth/**.

---

# 3. Creating JWT Tokens and Using Them to Secure Your RESTful APIs

Now that **Spring Security** is set up, let's focus on creating and using **JWT tokens** for securing our API.

### Creating JWT Token Utility Class

You will need a utility class to **generate** and **validate** JWT tokens. Here's an example of a class that generates a JWT token.

*import io.jsonwebtoken.Jwts;*

*import io.jsonwebtoken.SignatureAlgorithm;*

*import java.util.Date;*


*public class JwtTokenUtil {*


*private static final String SECRET_KEY = "mySecretKey"; // Secret key for signing JWT*


*public static String generateToken(String username) {*

*long expirationTime = 1000 * 60 * 60; // 1 hour*

```
return Jwts.builder()
        .setSubject(username)
        .setIssuedAt(new Date())
        .setExpiration(new Date(System.currentTimeMillis() +
expirationTime))
        .signWith(SignatureAlgorithm.HS256, SECRET_KEY)
        .compact();
    }
}
```

## Creating an Authentication Filter

You need to create a filter that will intercept each incoming request to check for a JWT token in the Authorization header and authenticate the user based on the token.

```
import io.jsonwebtoken.Jwts;
import org.springframework.security.core.Authentication;
import org.springframework.web.filter.OncePerRequestFilter;
import javax.servlet.Filter;
import javax.servlet.FilterChain;
import javax.servlet.ServletException;
import javax.servlet.http.HttpServletRequest;
import javax.servlet.http.HttpServletResponse;
import java.io.IOException;


public class JwtAuthenticationFilter extends OncePerRequestFilter {
```

```java
private static final String SECRET_KEY = "mySecretKey";

@Override
protected void doFilterInternal(HttpServletRequest request,
HttpServletResponse response, FilterChain filterChain)
    throws ServletException, IOException {

    String token = request.getHeader("Authorization");

    if (token != null && token.startsWith("Bearer ")) {
        String jwtToken = token.substring(7); // Extract the token
without "Bearer "
        String username = Jwts.parser()
                .setSigningKey(SECRET_KEY)
                .parseClaimsJws(jwtToken)
                .getBody()
                .getSubject();

        // Create authentication object and set it in the security
context
        Authentication authentication = new
UsernamePasswordAuthenticationToken(username, null, new
ArrayList<>());

SecurityContextHolder.getContext().setAuthentication(authenticatio
n);
    }
```

```
    filterChain.doFilter(request, response);
  }
}
```

## Registering the Filter in Security Configuration

Now, we need to register the JWT filter in our Spring Security configuration.

```
@Configuration
@EnableWebSecurity
public class SecurityConfig extends WebSecurityConfigurerAdapter
{

    @Autowired
    private JwtAuthenticationFilter jwtAuthenticationFilter;

    @Override
    protected void configure(HttpSecurity http) throws Exception {
      http.csrf().disable()
        .authorizeRequests()
        .antMatchers("/auth/**").permitAll() // Permit login and register
        .anyRequest().authenticated() // Authenticate all other requests
        .and()
        .addFilterBefore(jwtAuthenticationFilter,
UsernamePasswordAuthenticationFilter.class); // Add JWT filter
    }
}
```

# 4. Implementing Role-Based Access Control (RBAC) with JWT

Role-based access control (RBAC) allows you to restrict access to certain endpoints based on the roles of authenticated users.

### Adding Roles to JWT

You can add roles to the JWT token during generation:

```
public static String generateTokenWithRoles(String username,
String role) {

    long expirationTime = 1000 * 60 * 60; // 1 hour

    return Jwts.builder()
            .setSubject(username)
            .claim("role", role) // Add role to the token
            .setIssuedAt(new Date())
            .setExpiration(new Date(System.currentTimeMillis() +
expirationTime))
            .signWith(SignatureAlgorithm.HS256, SECRET_KEY)
            .compact();
}
```

### Securing Endpoints with Roles

In your SecurityConfig, you can restrict access to certain endpoints based on roles.

```
@Override
protected void configure(HttpSecurity http) throws Exception {
    http.csrf().disable()
```

```
.authorizeRequests()

.antMatchers("/auth/**").permitAll() // Public endpoints

.antMatchers("/admin/**").hasRole("ADMIN") // Only
accessible by ADMIN role

.anyRequest().authenticated()

.and()

.addFilterBefore(jwtAuthenticationFilter,
UsernamePasswordAuthenticationFilter.class);

}
```

This configuration ensures that only users with the **ADMIN** role can access the /admin/** endpoints.

---

# 5. Hands-On Project: Add JWT Authentication to Your To-Do List API and Implement Login/Logout Functionality

Let's apply what we've learned by adding **JWT authentication** to our **To-Do List API**. In this project, we'll implement **login** and **logout** functionality.

### Step 1: Set Up User Entity

We need a User entity to store user credentials and roles:

```
@Entity
public class User {


    @Id
    @GeneratedValue(strategy = GenerationType.IDENTITY)
    private Long id;
```

```java
private String username;

private String password;

private String role;

// Getters and Setters
}
```

## Step 2: Create Login Endpoint

Create a **login endpoint** that issues a JWT when users provide valid credentials:

```java
@RestController
@RequestMapping("/auth")
public class AuthController {

    @Autowired
    private UserService userService;

    @PostMapping("/login")
    public ResponseEntity<String> login(@RequestBody
LoginRequest loginRequest) {
```

```
    User user =
userService.authenticate(loginRequest.getUsername(),
loginRequest.getPassword());

    if (user != null) {

        String token =
JwtTokenUtil.generateTokenWithRoles(user.getUsername(),
user.getRole());

        return ResponseEntity.ok(token);

    }

    return
ResponseEntity.status(HttpStatus.UNAUTHORIZED).body("Invali
d credentials");

    }
}
```

## Step 3: Implement Logout (Optional)

JWT is **stateless**, so logout simply involves removing the token from the client side (typically from local storage or cookies). There's no server-side session to invalidate.

---

# Conclusion

In this chapter, you've learned how to secure your **Spring Boot APIs** using **JWT authentication**. You've seen how to create and validate JWT tokens, set up **Spring Security**, and implement **role-based access control (RBAC)** to restrict access to certain endpoints. Through a hands-on project, you added JWT authentication to your **To-Do List API** and implemented login functionality.

# Chapter 7: Microservices Architecture with Spring Boot

## Overview

In this chapter, we will explore the concept of **Microservices Architecture** and how to implement it using **Spring Boot**. You'll learn the foundational principles of microservices, the advantages and challenges associated with this architecture, and how to break down monolithic applications into smaller, independently deployable microservices.

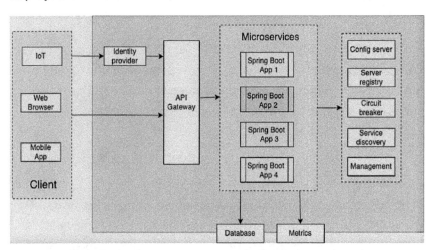

The goal of this chapter is not just to introduce microservices but to give you hands-on experience by refactoring your **To-Do List API** into multiple **microservices**. For example, we will create separate microservices for **Task Management** and **User Management**, making them interact seamlessly with each other.

## Key Topics Covered

1. **Introduction to Microservices Architecture**

2. **Advantages and Challenges of Microservices**

3. **Breaking Down Monolithic Applications into Microservices**

4. **Creating Multiple Spring Boot Services That Work Together**

5. **Hands-On Project: Refactor Your To-Do List API into Multiple Microservices, Such as Task Management and User Management Services**

# 1. Introduction to Microservices Architecture

## What Are Microservices?

**Microservices architecture** is an approach to software development where an application is built as a collection of small, independently deployable services. These services are loosely coupled and communicate with each other through lightweight protocols like **HTTP** or **messaging queues**.

In microservices, each service corresponds to a specific business function (like **User Management, Task Management**, or **Order Processing**) and can be developed, deployed, and scaled independently. This is in contrast to a **monolithic architecture**, where the entire application is tightly integrated into one large codebase.

## Key Characteristics of Microservices:

- **Independently Deployable**: Each microservice is a self-contained unit that can be developed, deployed, and scaled independently.

- **Small and Focused**: Each service handles a specific business function or domain, which makes the application more maintainable.

- **Communication via APIs**: Microservices communicate with each other through lightweight protocols (typically RESTful APIs or messaging systems).

- **Autonomous**: Each service has its own database and is independent of the other services' databases, which helps ensure loose coupling.

- **Technology Agnostic**: Microservices can be written in different programming languages, allowing teams to use the best tool for the job.

## How Microservices Work in Practice

Imagine you are building an online store. In a **monolithic architecture**, everything — from **user management** and **product catalog** to **order processing** and **payment systems** — would be bundled into a single application. The whole application is deployed as a single unit.

However, in a **microservices architecture**, each of these functions would be implemented as an individual microservice:

- **User Service**: Manages user data (registration, authentication, profile).

- **Product Service**: Manages the product catalog, inventory, and product details.

- **Order Service**: Handles customer orders and checkout processes.

- **Payment Service**: Manages payment processing.

Each of these services would interact with others via **APIs**. For example, when a user places an order, the **Order Service** will communicate with the **Product Service** to check inventory, and the **Payment Service** will process the payment.

---

# 2. Advantages and Challenges of Microservices

## Advantages of Microservices

1. **Scalability**: Each service can be scaled independently based on its needs. For example, the **Order Service** might need to be scaled up during peak shopping seasons, while the **User Service** may not require the same level of scaling.

2. **Flexibility**: Microservices allow teams to use different technologies for different services. One team can use **Spring Boot** and **Java**, while another might choose **Node.js** or **Python**, depending on the service's requirements.

3. **Resilience**: If one microservice fails, it doesn't bring down the entire application. Since services are independent, a failure in one service can be contained, preventing a **single point of failure**.

4. **Faster Development and Deployment**: Teams can work independently on different services, speeding up development. Services can be deployed independently, allowing for continuous integration and delivery (CI/CD).

5. **Easier Maintenance**: Since each microservice is focused on a single responsibility, it's easier to maintain and update. Changes can be made to one service without affecting the entire system.

## Challenges of Microservices

1. **Complexity**: Managing multiple services can be complex. It involves handling **service discovery, inter-service communication**, and **data consistency**.

2. **Network Latency**: Since services communicate over the network, there might be performance overhead due to network latency. Proper optimization and efficient communication are essential.

3. **Data Management**: In a monolithic architecture, a single database often handles all the data. With microservices, each service may have its own database, and maintaining consistency across these databases can be challenging.

4. **Distributed Tracing**: Debugging and monitoring become more complex when an issue spans multiple services. Tools like **Spring Cloud** and **Zipkin** can help with distributed tracing.

5. **Deployment and Monitoring**: Managing multiple services requires robust deployment pipelines and monitoring solutions to ensure everything is running smoothly.

# 3. Breaking Down Monolithic Applications into Microservices

One of the main reasons for adopting microservices is to break down **monolithic applications** into manageable pieces. Here's how you can approach the transition:

## Steps to Break Down a Monolith

1. **Identify Core Domains**: Start by identifying the different **business domains** in your application. For example, in an e-commerce application, domains could include **user management**, **product catalog**, and **order processing**.

2. **Create Independent Services**: Extract each domain into its own **microservice**. Each service should be responsible for a single business function and should have its own **data storage**.

3. **Define Clear Interfaces**: Services should interact with each other via well-defined APIs. Make sure to use lightweight communication protocols like **RESTful APIs** or **message brokers**.

4. **Handle Data Consistency**: In microservices, each service has its own database. Ensure that **data consistency** is maintained using patterns like **event-driven architecture** or **sagas**.

5. **Refactor Incrementally**: Start by extracting one or two functionalities as microservices, leaving the rest in the monolith. Gradually refactor the monolith as new services are created.

# 4. Creating Multiple Spring Boot Services That Work Together

Now that you understand the principles of microservices, let's explore how to create multiple **Spring Boot services** and make them work together.

## Creating a Microservice

Here's a simple guide to creating a microservice in Spring Boot:

1.  **Set Up Spring Boot Project**: Go to Spring Initializr and create a new Spring Boot project for your microservice. Add dependencies like **Spring Web, Spring Data JPA,** and your preferred database driver.

2.  **Create a Service Class**: Define a service that performs business logic.

```java
@Service
public class TaskService {

    private final TaskRepository taskRepository;

    @Autowired
    public TaskService(TaskRepository taskRepository) {
        this.taskRepository = taskRepository;
    }

    public Task createTask(Task task) {
        return taskRepository.save(task);
    }
```

```
public List<Task> getAllTasks() {
    return taskRepository.findAll();
  }
}
```

3. **Create a REST Controller:** Create a controller to expose the service via HTTP.

```
@RestController
@RequestMapping("/tasks")
public class TaskController {

  private final TaskService taskService;

  @Autowired
  public TaskController(TaskService taskService) {
    this.taskService = taskService;
  }

  @PostMapping
  public Task createTask(@RequestBody Task task) {
    return taskService.createTask(task);
  }

  @GetMapping
  public List<Task> getAllTasks() {
```

```
return taskService.getAllTasks();
    }
}
```

4. **Run the Application**: Use **./mvnw spring-boot:run** to start the microservice.

---

## Inter-Service Communication

One of the most important parts of microservices is how the services communicate with each other. For our To-Do List API, we'll implement a **User Service** and a **Task Service**.

1. **Task Service** will manage tasks (as we created earlier).

2. **User Service** will manage user data, such as registration and authentication.

To allow the services to communicate with each other, we will use **RESTful APIs**. The **User Service** will send HTTP requests to the **Task Service** to create or fetch tasks.

---

# 5. Hands-On Project: Refactor Your To-Do List API into Multiple Microservices (Task Management and User Management)

### Step 1: Create the User Service

## Create a User Entity:

```
@Entity
public class User {
```

```java
@Id
@GeneratedValue(strategy = GenerationType.IDENTITY)
private Long id;

private String username;
private String password;

// Getters and Setters
}
```

**Create the User Repository:**

```
public interface UserRepository extends JpaRepository<User, Long> {

    Optional<User> findByUsername(String username);
}
```

**Create the User Service:**

```
@Service
public class UserService {

    private final UserRepository userRepository;

    @Autowired
    public UserService(UserRepository userRepository) {
        this.userRepository = userRepository;
    }

    public User registerUser(User user) {
        return userRepository.save(user);
    }

    public Optional<User> findByUsername(String username) {
        return userRepository.findByUsername(username);
    }
}
```

## Create the User Controller:

```
@RestController
@RequestMapping("/users")
public class UserController {

    private final UserService userService;

    @Autowired
    public UserController(UserService userService) {
        this.userService = userService;
    }

    @PostMapping("/register")
    public User register(@RequestBody User user) {
        return userService.registerUser(user);
    }

    @GetMapping("/{username}")
    public User getUser(@PathVariable String username) {
        return userService.findByUsername(username)
                .orElseThrow(() -> new RuntimeException("User
not found"));
    }
}
```

**Step 2: Create the Task Service**

1. **Task Entity** (as previously defined).

2. **Task Repository** (as previously defined).

3. **Task Service** (as previously defined).

4. **Task Controller** (as previously defined).

---

## Step 3: Service Communication

To allow the **Task Service** to communicate with the **User Service**, we can use **RESTful API calls**.

In the **Task Service**, we'll send HTTP requests to the **User Service** to check if a user exists before creating a task.

```
@Service
public class TaskService {

    private final TaskRepository taskRepository;
    private final RestTemplate restTemplate;

    @Autowired
    public TaskService(TaskRepository taskRepository,
RestTemplate restTemplate) {
        this.taskRepository = taskRepository;
        this.restTemplate = restTemplate;
    }

    public Task createTask(Task task, String username) {
```

```
// Call User Service to verify if user exists

User user = restTemplate.getForObject("http://user-
service/users/{username}", User.class, username);

if (user != null) {

    return taskRepository.save(task);

}

throw new RuntimeException("User not found");

}

}
```

## Step 4: Test the Microservices

1. **Run Both Services**: Start both the **User Service** and **Task Service** on different ports.

2. **Test the Task Service**: Using **Postman**, send a **POST** request to /tasks with task details and a valid username.

# Conclusion

In this chapter, you learned how to transition from a **monolithic application** to a **microservices architecture** using **Spring Boot**. You explored the benefits of microservices, as well as the challenges they introduce. Through hands-on examples, you broke down your **To-Do List API** into separate services for **Task Management** and **User Management**.

# Chapter 8: Communication Between Microservices with RESTful APIs

## Overview

As we continue our journey with **microservices**, one crucial aspect is how these services **communicate** with each other. Microservices work in isolation but need to share data and perform operations that require **inter-service communication**. This chapter focuses on the **communication between microservices** using **RESTful APIs**.

In this chapter, you will learn:

- **How microservices communicate** via **REST APIs**.

- How to **create RESTful endpoints** in Spring Boot to facilitate inter-service communication.

- How to **consume REST APIs** from other services using **RestTemplate** and **WebClient**.

By the end of this chapter, you'll have a clear understanding of how to integrate and manage communication between your microservices, and we'll walk through a hands-on project where we create communication between a **Task Management** service and a **User Management** service using RESTful APIs.

---

### Key Topics Covered

1. **Introduction to RESTful Communication Between Services**

2. **Creating REST Endpoints for Communication**

3. **Consuming REST APIs Using RestTemplate or WebClient**

4. **Hands-On Project: Create Communication Between Task Management and User Management Services Using REST APIs**

---

# 1. Introduction to RESTful Communication Between Services

Microservices often need to interact with each other to complete tasks that span multiple services. In the context of **microservices architecture**, communication typically occurs over a **network**. Since microservices are usually distributed systems, it's essential that they communicate in a way that is both efficient and standardized.

## What Is RESTful Communication?

**REST (Representational State Transfer)** is an architectural style for designing networked applications. When you use **RESTful communication**, your services communicate over HTTP and exchange **data** in a **stateless** manner. This makes **REST** an ideal choice for microservices communication, as it is simple, lightweight, and scalable.

In REST, communication between services occurs through **HTTP methods** (like GET, POST, PUT, DELETE), where each service exposes specific **REST endpoints** to which other services can make requests.

## Key Benefits of RESTful Communication:

1. **Statelessness**: Each request is independent. The client sends all the necessary information (authentication, data) in the request, so no session information is stored on the server.

2. **Scalability**: RESTful APIs are scalable since they follow simple HTTP protocols and are often cached at different points (e.g., client-side, server-side, reverse proxy).

3. **Flexibility**: REST allows multiple data formats like **JSON** or **XML**, but **JSON** is the most commonly used format due to its simplicity.

---

## Communication Patterns in Microservices

There are several ways microservices communicate:

1. **Synchronous Communication (REST API)**:

   o Services send **HTTP requests** and wait for the response before proceeding.

   o **Example**: A User Service calls the Task Service to retrieve a list of tasks for a user.

2. **Asynchronous Communication (Message Queues)**:

   o Services communicate via **message queues** or **event-driven systems** like **Kafka** or **RabbitMQ**, which decouples services and allows them to operate independently.

   o **Example**: An Order Service sends an event message that a new order has been placed, and a Payment Service subscribes to the event to process payment.

For this chapter, we will focus on **synchronous communication** via **RESTful APIs**.

# 2. Creating REST Endpoints for Communication

## Setting Up a Microservice with REST Endpoints

Let's start by creating the **Task Management Service** and **User Management Service**. The services will expose **RESTful endpoints** for communication. We'll begin by creating a simple **User Service** and a **Task Service** using **Spring Boot**.

## Step 1: Creating the User Service

The **User Service** will manage the users of the system, providing a way to fetch and manage user data.

1. **Create the User Entity:**

```java
@Entity
public class User {

    @Id
    @GeneratedValue(strategy = GenerationType.IDENTITY)
    private Long id;

    private String username;
    private String password;
```

```
// Constructor, getters, and setters
}
```

## Create the User Repository:

```
public interface UserRepository extends JpaRepository<User,
Long> {

    Optional<User> findByUsername(String username);
}
```

## Create the User Service:

```
@Service
public class UserService {

    @Autowired
    private UserRepository userRepository;

    public User createUser(User user) {
        return userRepository.save(user);
    }

    public User getUserByUsername(String username) {
        return userRepository.findByUsername(username)
                .orElseThrow(() -> new RuntimeException("User
not found"));
    }
}
```

### 4. Create the User Controller:

```
@RestController
```

```
@RequestMapping("/users")
public class UserController {

    @Autowired
    private UserService userService;

    @PostMapping("/register")
    public User registerUser(@RequestBody User user) {
        return userService.createUser(user);
    }

    @GetMapping("/{username}")
    public User getUserByUsername(@PathVariable String
username) {
        return userService.getUserByUsername(username);
    }
}
```

---

## Step 2: Creating the Task Service

Now, let's create the **Task Service** which will manage tasks.

1. **Create the Task Entity:**

```
@Entity
public class Task {

    @Id
```

```
@GeneratedValue(strategy = GenerationType.IDENTITY)
private Long id;

private String description;

// Constructor, getters, and setters
}
```

2. **Create the Task Repository:**

```
public interface TaskRepository extends JpaRepository<Task,
Long> {
    List<Task> findByDescription(String description);
}
```

3. **Create the Task Service:**

```
@Service
public class TaskService {

    @Autowired
    private TaskRepository taskRepository;

    public Task createTask(Task task) {
        return taskRepository.save(task);
    }

    public List<Task> getAllTasks() {
        return taskRepository.findAll();
```

```
    }
}
```

### 4. Create the Task Controller:

```
@RestController
@RequestMapping("/tasks")
public class TaskController {

    @Autowired
    private TaskService taskService;

    @PostMapping
    public Task createTask(@RequestBody Task task) {
        return taskService.createTask(task);
    }

    @GetMapping
    public List<Task> getAllTasks() {
        return taskService.getAllTasks();
    }
}
```

Now, you have two independent services: **UserService** and **TaskService,** each exposing RESTful endpoints. These services can communicate with each other using **RESTful APIs.**

# 3. Consuming REST APIs Using RestTemplate or WebClient

In a microservices environment, services need to **consume** REST APIs provided by other services. There are two main ways to achieve this in Spring Boot:

- **RestTemplate**: An older, synchronous API for consuming RESTful services.

- **WebClient**: A more modern, non-blocking, and asynchronous API that is part of **Spring WebFlux**.

## Using RestTemplate

RestTemplate Configuration:

To use RestTemplate, you need to define a **bean** in your configuration.

```
@Configuration
public class AppConfig {

    @Bean
    public RestTemplate restTemplate() {
        return new RestTemplate();
    }
}
```

Consuming REST APIs with RestTemplate:

Let's update the **TaskService** to consume the **UserService** API using **RestTemplate**.

```java
@Service
public class TaskService {

    @Autowired
    private RestTemplate restTemplate;

    @Autowired
    private TaskRepository taskRepository;

    public Task createTask(Task task, String username) {
        // Fetch user data from User Service
        User user = restTemplate.getForObject("http://user-service/users/{username}", User.class, username);

        if (user != null) {
            task.setDescription("Task for user: " + user.getUsername());
            return taskRepository.save(task);
        }

        throw new RuntimeException("User not found");
    }
}
```

In the above code, the **TaskService** calls the **UserService** via the RestTemplate to fetch user details based on the username, then creates a task for that user.

## Using WebClient (Recommended)

WebClient is the recommended approach for making **asynchronous** and **non-blocking** HTTP requests. It is more efficient and can handle large numbers of concurrent requests.

1. **WebClient Configuration**:

To use WebClient, first add the required dependency to your **pom.xml**:

```xml
<dependency>
    <groupId>org.springframework.boot</groupId>
    <artifactId>spring-boot-starter-webflux</artifactId>
</dependency>
```

Then, define a WebClient bean in your configuration:

```java
@Configuration
public class WebClientConfig {

    @Bean
    public WebClient.Builder webClientBuilder() {
        return WebClient.builder();
    }
}
```

2. **Consuming REST APIs with WebClient**:

Now, let's update the **TaskService** to use **WebClient**.

```java
@Service
public class TaskService {
```

```
@Autowired
private WebClient.Builder webClientBuilder;

@Autowired
private TaskRepository taskRepository;

public Task createTask(Task task, String username) {
    // Fetch user data from User Service
    User user = webClientBuilder.baseUrl("http://user-service")
                    .get()
                    .uri("/users/{username}", username)
                    .retrieve()
                    .bodyToMono(User.class)
                    .block();

    if (user != null) {
        task.setDescription("Task for user: " + user.getUsername());
        return taskRepository.save(task);
    }

    throw new RuntimeException("User not found");
    }
}
```

In this example, **WebClient** asynchronously retrieves user data from the **UserService.** The bodyToMono(User.class) converts the response into a Mono<User>, and block() waits for the result synchronously (although block() is typically not used in asynchronous applications, it's fine for our use case here).

---

# 4. Hands-On Project: Create Communication Between Task Management and User Management Services Using REST APIs

Now, let's put everything together. We'll extend the **To-Do List API** into two services: **Task Management** and **User Management**, and ensure they can communicate using **RESTful APIs**.

### Step 1: Create the User Management Service

We've already created the **UserService** and **UserController**. Ensure that the UserService is running independently on a different port, say **8081**.

### Step 2: Create the Task Management Service

We've also created the **TaskService** and **TaskController**. Update the **TaskService** to consume the **UserService** via either **RestTemplate** or **WebClient**.

### Step 3: Service Communication via RestTemplate/WebClient

- The **Task Service** should call the **User Service** to verify if a user exists before creating a task.

- Use **RestTemplate** or **WebClient** to fetch the user data from the **User Service**.

### Step 4: Test the Communication

1. Start the **User Service** and **Task Service** on different ports (8081 for **User Service** and 8080 for **Task Service**).

2. Use **Postman** to test the **Task Service**:

   o  Send a **POST** request to /tasks with a task description and a valid username.

---

# Conclusion

In this chapter, you learned how to implement **RESTful communication** between microservices using **Spring Boot**. We explored how to create **REST endpoints** and how to **consume REST APIs** using **RestTemplate** and **WebClient**. You also gained hands-on experience by implementing communication between two microservices: **Task Management** and **User Management**.

# Chapter 9: Working with Databases in a Microservices Environment

## Overview

In a **microservices architecture**, managing databases is an important aspect of ensuring your services are scalable, maintainable, and independent. Unlike monolithic applications where a single database is used, in microservices, each service often manages its own **database**. This approach, known as **Database per Service** (DbS), allows each microservice to be fully autonomous in terms of data management, making it easier to scale and modify each service independently.

In this chapter, we'll dive deep into how to manage **databases in a microservices environment**, focusing on decentralized data management, database configuration, and ensuring data consistency across services. We'll also provide a **hands-on project** where you'll set up separate databases for each service in your To-Do List application.

---

### Key Topics Covered

1. **Database per Service Pattern and Decentralized Data Management**

2. **Configuring Data Sources for Each Microservice**

3. **Implementing Inter-Service Communication with Database Synchronization**

4. **Hands-On Project: Set Up Separate Databases for Task Management and User Management**

---

# 1. Database per Service Pattern and Decentralized Data Management

### What is the Database per Service Pattern?

The **Database per Service** pattern is a fundamental principle in microservices architecture. It dictates that each microservice should have its own **database**, thus ensuring that it remains **autonomous** and **loosely coupled** with other services. This means that each service is responsible for its own data storage and retrieval, and there is no central database shared between services.

### Advantages of Database per Service:

1. **Independence**: Each service can evolve and scale independently, without being dependent on a shared database schema.

2. **Decoupling**: The data storage of one service does not affect the other, ensuring that changes to one service's database won't impact others.

3. **Optimized for Each Service**: Each service can use the most appropriate database technology (e.g., SQL, NoSQL) that fits its needs. For example, a **User Service** might use **PostgreSQL** for relational data, while a **Task Service** might use **MongoDB** for document-based data.

4. **Scalability**: Since each service is independent, it can be scaled independently based on its own database requirements.

## Challenges of Database per Service:

1. **Data Duplication**: Since each service has its own database, there may be some duplication of data across services, leading to potential consistency issues.

2. **Data Synchronization**: Ensuring that data is consistent across microservices becomes a challenge, especially when one service's data is required by another.

3. **Distributed Transactions**: Traditional database transactions, which ensure consistency across tables within a single database, are harder to implement across multiple databases. This is often addressed through **event-driven architectures** or **saga patterns**.

## Data Management in Microservices: Decentralization

Microservices rely on **decentralized data management**, where each service owns and manages its own data. This decentralization is achieved through:

1. **Independent Databases**: Each service has its own database, with no sharing of schema or data.

2. **Asynchronous Communication**: Services typically communicate via asynchronous mechanisms such as **event-driven architectures** or **message queues** (e.g., **Kafka, RabbitMQ**).

3. **Data Ownership**: A service is the sole owner of the data it manages, ensuring that no other service can modify its data directly.

4. **Eventual Consistency**: Rather than guaranteeing **immediate consistency** (like in a monolithic architecture),

microservices often rely on **eventual consistency**, ensuring that data across services is synchronized over time.

# 2. Configuring Data Sources for Each Microservice

Now, let's walk through how to **configure separate databases** for each microservice in a Spring Boot environment. We'll be working with two services in our **To-Do List API**: a **Task Management** service and a **User Management** service.

### Setting Up the Databases

1. **Task Management Service Database**: For simplicity, let's assume we're using **PostgreSQL** for the Task Management service.

2. **User Management Service Database**: The **User Management** service will use **MySQL**.

We will configure each microservice with its own **data source** and ensure they operate independently.

### Step 1: Configure Data Source for Task Service (PostgreSQL)

In the application.properties file of the **Task Service**, we will configure the **PostgreSQL** database connection:

```
# Task Service Database Configuration (PostgreSQL)
spring.datasource.url=jdbc:postgresql://localhost:5432/task_db
spring.datasource.username=postgres
spring.datasource.password=password
```

*spring.jpa.hibernate.ddl-auto=update*

*spring.jpa.show-sql=true*

*spring.jpa.database-platform=org.hibernate.dialect.PostgreSQL95Dialect*

- **spring.datasource.url**: Specifies the connection string to the PostgreSQL database.

- **spring.jpa.hibernate.ddl-auto**: Set to update to auto-generate the database schema based on entities.

- **spring.jpa.show-sql**: Logs the SQL queries for debugging purposes.

---

### Step 2: Configure Data Source for User Service (MySQL)

In the application.properties file of the **User Service**, we will configure the **MySQL** database connection:

*# User Service Database Configuration (MySQL)*

*spring.datasource.url=jdbc:mysql://localhost:3306/user_db*

*spring.datasource.username=root*

*spring.datasource.password=rootpassword*

*spring.jpa.hibernate.ddl-auto=update*

*spring.jpa.show-sql=true*

*spring.jpa.database-platform=org.hibernate.dialect.MySQL5InnoDBDialect*

This configuration is similar to the **Task Service** database configuration, except it connects to a **MySQL** database instead of **PostgreSQL**.

---

## Step 3: Define the Entity and Repository for Each Service

In both services, we define **entities** and **repositories** for interacting with the database.

### Task Entity and Repository (Task Service)

```
@Entity
public class Task {

    @Id
    @GeneratedValue(strategy = GenerationType.IDENTITY)
    private Long id;

    private String description;

    // Getters and Setters
}


public interface TaskRepository extends JpaRepository<Task, Long> {
    List<Task> findByDescription(String description);
}
```

### User Entity and Repository (User Service)

```
@Entity
public class User {

    @Id
```

```
@GeneratedValue(strategy = GenerationType.IDENTITY)
private Long id;

private String username;
private String password;

// Getters and Setters
}


public interface UserRepository extends JpaRepository<User,
Long> {
    Optional<User> findByUsername(String username);
}
```

---

# 3. Implementing Inter-Service Communication with Database Synchronization

Once our databases are set up and the services are configured, we need to ensure that data is consistent across these microservices. Microservices often use **asynchronous communication** and **event-driven patterns** to achieve synchronization. We'll look at how to implement **RESTful communication** between services to handle **inter-service data synchronization**.

### Step 1: Communicating Between Services Using REST

Let's create communication between the **User Management Service** and the **Task Management Service** using **REST APIs**.

**Calling the User Service from the Task Service**

In the **Task Service**, we can use **RestTemplate** or **WebClient** to communicate with the **User Service**.

1. **Add RestTemplate to Task Service**: First, configure **RestTemplate** in the **Task Service** configuration.

```
@Configuration
public class AppConfig {

  @Bean
  public RestTemplate restTemplate() {
    return new RestTemplate();
  }
}
```

2. **Consume User Service API in Task Service**: Now, in the **TaskService**, we will call the **UserService** to verify if a user exists before creating a task.

```
@Service
public class TaskService {

  @Autowired
  private RestTemplate restTemplate;

  @Autowired
  private TaskRepository taskRepository;
```

```
public Task createTask(Task task, String username) {
    // Call the User Service to verify if the user exists
    User user =
restTemplate.getForObject("http://localhost:8081/users/{username}",
User.class, username);

    if (user != null) {
        task.setDescription("Task for user: " + user.getUsername());
        return taskRepository.save(task);
    }

    throw new RuntimeException("User not found");
  }
}
```

In this example, **RestTemplate** is used to make a GET request to the **UserService** to verify if a user exists based on the username.

## Step 2: Data Synchronization

In a **distributed microservices** environment, data synchronization becomes a challenge when data from one service needs to be reflected in another service. You could implement **synchronous communication** via REST APIs, or use **event-driven communication** using message queues (e.g., **Kafka** or **RabbitMQ**).

In this case, we will stick with **synchronous communication** for simplicity, but for more advanced architectures, you might consider an **event-driven architecture** for better decoupling.

# 4. Hands-On Project: Set Up Separate Databases for Task Management and User Management

### Step 1: Set Up the User Service

1. **Create the User Entity** (as shown earlier).

2. **Create the User Repository** (as shown earlier).

3. **Create the User Service** and **User Controller** (as shown earlier).

4. **Run the User Service** on **port 8081**.

### Step 2: Set Up the Task Service

1. **Create the Task Entity** (as shown earlier).

2. **Create the Task Repository** (as shown earlier).

3. **Create the Task Service** and **Task Controller** (as shown earlier).

4. **Use RestTemplate to Communicate with the User Service** (as shown earlier).

5. **Run the Task Service** on **port 8080**.

### Step 3: Test the Services

1. **Run Both Services:** Start both the **User Service** (on port 8081) and **Task Service** (on port 8080).

2. **Create Users:** Use **Postman** or **cURL** to make **POST** requests to /users/register and create users.

3. **Create Tasks:** Use **Postman** or **cURL** to make **POST** requests to /tasks and associate tasks with users.

### Step 4: Validate Data Synchronization

Test the communication between the services by creating a user and a task. Ensure that the **Task Service** is able to retrieve user details from the **User Service** and create tasks accordingly.

---

# Conclusion

In this chapter, you learned how to manage **databases in a microservices environment** using the **Database per Service** pattern. We explored how to **configure separate databases** for each microservice and discussed the challenges of decentralized data management.

You also learned how to implement **RESTful communication** between services, allowing them to interact and synchronize data. With this foundation, you're well on your way to building scalable and maintainable microservices that manage their own data independently.

# Chapter 10: Managing API Versioning and Forward Compatibility

## Overview

In today's rapidly evolving digital landscape, software applications frequently undergo updates and changes. This results in a critical need for managing **API versioning** to ensure that users of your API can continue to work seamlessly with previous versions while also benefiting from new features in the latest releases.

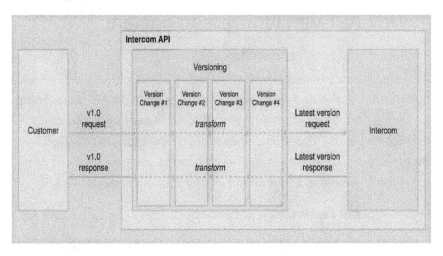

In this chapter, we will explore the concept of **API versioning**—why it's essential, the different strategies for versioning your APIs, and how to ensure that your APIs remain **forward-compatible**. We'll also focus on how to implement versioning in your **To-Do List API**, ensuring that you can introduce changes without breaking existing user applications.

Key Topics Covered

1. **Why API Versioning is Important**

2. **Different Strategies for API Versioning (URL Path Versioning, Query Parameters, Headers)**

3. **Handling Backward Compatibility**

4. **Hands-On Project: Implement API Versioning in Your To-Do List API and Handle Changes Without Breaking Existing Users**

# 1. Why API Versioning is Important

## The Need for API Versioning

APIs are the backbone of most modern web applications. As businesses evolve and new features are added to an API, **versioning** becomes necessary to prevent breaking changes that could affect existing clients. Without proper versioning, developers may find themselves stuck between the need to introduce new features and the need to maintain compatibility with older versions of the API.

Here's why **API versioning** is essential:

1. **Backward Compatibility**: When you update an API, you risk breaking existing client applications. Proper versioning ensures that old clients can still interact with your API without breaking.

2. **API Evolution**: As software grows, its functionality expands. Versioning allows you to evolve your API by adding new

features without removing or altering existing functionality that users rely on.

3. **Decoupling Client and Server**: API versioning provides a way to decouple client and server evolution. Clients can continue using older versions of an API, while servers can introduce new features and bug fixes.

4. **Clear Communication**: Versioning provides clear communication with users of the API about which version they are interacting with and which features are available.

## Different Types of Changes and Their Impact on Clients

When a new feature is added, or an existing one is modified, it can lead to the following:

1. **Non-Breaking Changes (Backward Compatible)**: These changes add new functionality or features without changing or removing existing ones.

   o Example: Adding a new optional field to a response.

2. **Breaking Changes**: These changes alter or remove existing functionality, causing problems for clients who rely on the old behavior.

   o Example: Removing or renaming an existing API endpoint or field in the response.

## The Risks of Not Using API Versioning

Without proper versioning, developers risk creating **fragile APIs** that can lead to:

- **Broken integrations**: Clients may fail to work as expected, resulting in poor user experience.

- **Hard-to-maintain code**: As APIs evolve without proper versioning, managing changes becomes increasingly complex.

- **Difficulty with backward compatibility**: New versions of APIs may unintentionally break old clients if not handled carefully.

By implementing versioning, you ensure that your API can evolve while maintaining the stability and reliability of existing services.

---

# 2. Different Strategies for API Versioning

When it comes to implementing versioning in your API, there are several strategies. The strategy you choose will depend on your API's needs, your users' preferences, and how much control you want over versioning.

## 1. URL Path Versioning

URL path versioning is one of the most common methods for versioning APIs. In this strategy, the version of the API is specified in the URL path, making it explicit for clients.

**Example:**

https://api.yourapp.com/v1/tasks

https://api.yourapp.com/v2/tasks

Here, v1 and v2 represent different versions of the API. Clients can simply change the version number in the URL path to switch between different versions of the API.

**Advantages:**

- **Clear and explicit**: Versioning is visible and immediately clear in the URL.

- **Easy to manage**: You can maintain separate controllers and mappings for each version.

**Disadvantages:**

- **May cause redundancy**: If the changes between versions are small, having multiple endpoints for each version could lead to redundant code.

- **Requires clients to manually update versions**: Clients need to modify the URL when moving to a new version.

---

## 2. Query Parameter Versioning

With query parameter versioning, you can include the version number as a query parameter in the URL.

**Example:**

https://api.yourapp.com/tasks?version=1

https://api.yourapp.com/tasks?version=2

This allows clients to specify which version of the API they want to use through a simple query parameter.

**Advantages:**

- **Less intrusive**: You don't need to change the base URL structure, making it less disruptive for existing clients.

- **Flexible**: It's easy to modify and test multiple versions without changing your URL structure.

**Disadvantages:**

- **Less explicit**: The version is not immediately visible in the URL path, making it harder to track versions.

- **Potential for confusion**: Users may forget to specify the version in the query parameters, leading to unintended behavior.

---

## 3. Header Versioning

With header-based versioning, the version number is passed in the HTTP header instead of the URL. This method allows for clean URLs but requires additional setup to handle versioning in headers.

**Example:**

*GET /tasks*

*Headers:*

*X-API-Version: 1*

This approach relies on custom headers (e.g., X-API-Version) to specify which version of the API is being requested.

**Advantages:**

- **Clean URLs**: The URL path doesn't have to include versioning information, keeping the URL structure simple and clean.

- **Flexibility**: Versioning can be managed in the headers without affecting the URL or query parameters.

**Disadvantages:**

- **Less visibility**: The version is not visible in the URL, which could make debugging and tracking versions more challenging.

- **Requires custom logic**: You need to configure your server to handle custom headers, which could introduce complexity.

## 4. Accept Header Versioning

Accept header versioning is similar to header versioning, but the version information is included in the **Accept** header.

**Example**:

*GET /tasks*

*Accept: application/vnd.yourapp.v1+json*

This approach uses custom MIME types in the **Accept** header to specify the API version.

**Advantages**:

- **Separation of concerns**: The versioning information is kept out of the URL entirely, which is clean and neat.

**Disadvantages**:

- **Requires client support**: Clients need to send a custom Accept header, which might not be supported by all libraries or frameworks.

- **Less visibility**: Like header versioning, this approach makes it harder to track the version directly from the URL.

# 3. Handling Backward Compatibility

While introducing new versions of an API, you must ensure that your previous versions continue to work smoothly for existing clients. This is known as **backward compatibility**.

## What is Backward Compatibility?

**Backward compatibility** means that clients using an older version of the API should still be able to make requests and receive valid responses, even if the API has evolved. It ensures that existing functionality is not disrupted by new changes, and clients don't need to make changes every time a new version of the API is released.

## Strategies to Maintain Backward Compatibility:

1. **Additive Changes**: Adding new features, optional fields, or endpoints that don't affect existing functionality. This can be done without breaking backward compatibility.

   o   Example: Adding a new **optional field** in the response.

2. **Deprecation Strategy**: If a feature is removed, it should be deprecated first, giving users time to migrate to the new version.

   o   Example: Marking an endpoint as **deprecated** in the response headers.

3. **Non-Breaking Changes**: Avoid changing the structure of existing responses, especially for fields that clients depend on.

   o   Example: Changing an internal field name (without breaking the external API contract).

4. **Versioned Endpoints**: Keep the old versions active for a period, allowing users to migrate to newer versions at their own pace.

   o Example: Allow both v1 and v2 endpoints to coexist.

---

# 4. Hands-On Project: Implement API Versioning in Your To-Do List API and Handle Changes Without Breaking Existing Users

In this section, we'll implement **API versioning** in your **To-Do List API** and ensure backward compatibility by using **URL path versioning**.

## Step 1: Define Versioned Endpoints for Task Management

In the **Task Service**, we'll define two versions of the **TaskController**.

1. **Version 1 (v1) of TaskController:**

```
@RestController
@RequestMapping("/v1/tasks")
public class TaskControllerV1 {

    @Autowired
    private TaskService taskService;

    @PostMapping
    public Task createTask(@RequestBody Task task) {
        return taskService.createTask(task);
```

```
}

@GetMapping
public List<Task> getAllTasks() {
    return taskService.getAllTasks();
}
}
```

2. **Version 2 (v2) of TaskController** with new fields or methods:

```
@RestController
@RequestMapping("/v2/tasks")
public class TaskControllerV2 {

    @Autowired
    private TaskService taskService;

    @PostMapping
    public Task createTaskV2(@RequestBody Task task) {
        task.setDescription(task.getDescription().toUpperCase()); //
New logic for v2
        return taskService.createTask(task);
    }

    @GetMapping
    public List<Task> getAllTasks() {
        return taskService.getAllTasks();
    }
```

## Step 2: Update API Documentation

Add **documentation** to inform users about the changes in version 2 and how they can migrate.

- Provide an example of the new response format for **v2**.

- Clearly mark deprecated features in **v1** if necessary.

## Step 3: Implement Backward Compatibility

Ensure that **v1** continues to function for existing clients while introducing new features in **v2**. You can implement **additive changes** in **v2**, such as new fields in the response or extra functionality, without affecting **v1**.

## Step 4: Test the Versioning

1. **Test Version 1**: Ensure that clients using v1 endpoints still work as expected.

2. **Test Version 2**: Ensure that the new version (v2) works correctly and incorporates new features without breaking old functionality.

3. **Ensure Compatibility**: Make sure that **both versions** can coexist without issues.

---

## Conclusion

In this chapter, you learned about **API versioning**—its importance, the different strategies available, and how to ensure **backward compatibility** when evolving your APIs. Through a hands-on project, you implemented **versioned endpoints** in the **To-Do List API** using **URL path versioning**, ensuring that both old and new clients can use the service.

You also learned how to handle **backward compatibility** by using **additive changes, deprecation strategies,** and maintaining different versions of your API simultaneously. As you continue building your applications, effective versioning ensures that your APIs remain **flexible, scalable,** and **user-friendly.**

# Chapter 11: Building Scalable and Resilient Microservices with Spring Cloud

## Overview

Microservices have revolutionized how we build scalable and resilient distributed applications. However, building such systems often introduces complexity, especially as the number of services grows. Managing these services, ensuring they can communicate with each other, and maintaining fault tolerance becomes crucial.

This chapter introduces **Spring Cloud,** a framework designed to simplify the building of **scalable, resilient,** and **distributed microservices.** We'll explore how to leverage Spring Cloud's various tools to tackle common challenges in microservices architecture, such as:

- Centralized configuration management using **Spring Cloud Config.**

- **Service discovery** with **Eureka** to make services discoverable and scalable.

- **Fault tolerance** and **resilience patterns** with **Hystrix** to keep your services running even when one fails.

By the end of this chapter, you'll integrate **Spring Cloud** into your existing microservices architecture, making your system more robust, fault-tolerant, and scalable.

---

### Key Topics Covered

1. **Introduction to Spring Cloud for Distributed Systems**

2. **Using Spring Cloud Config for Centralized Configuration Management**

3. **Implementing Service Discovery with Eureka**

4. **Handling Fault Tolerance with Hystrix and Resilience Patterns**

5. **Hands-On Project: Integrating Spring Cloud into Your Microservices Architecture for Service Discovery and Resilience**

---

# 1. Introduction to Spring Cloud for Distributed Systems

### What is Spring Cloud?

**Spring Cloud** is a suite of tools that simplifies building **distributed systems** using the Spring ecosystem. When working with microservices, you encounter several complexities such as service discovery, configuration management, fault tolerance, load balancing, and monitoring. **Spring Cloud** provides solutions to all these challenges, making it easier to develop and deploy **resilient**, **scalable**, and **fault-tolerant microservices**.

Spring Cloud works seamlessly with **Spring Boot**, providing a set of tools that integrate well with microservices-based architecture, enabling:

- **Centralized Configuration**: Managing configuration for all services in one place.

- **Service Discovery**: Enabling services to find and communicate with each other.

- **Load Balancing**: Distributing requests efficiently across services.

- **Fault Tolerance**: Ensuring that the system remains operational even when individual services fail.

## Key Components of Spring Cloud

1. **Spring Cloud Config**: Provides centralized configuration management for distributed applications.

2. **Spring Cloud Netflix Eureka**: A service discovery tool that enables services to register themselves and discover other services.

3. **Spring Cloud Netflix Hystrix**: A library for adding fault tolerance to your microservices.

4. **Spring Cloud Gateway**: A gateway for routing requests to microservices.

5. **Spring Cloud Stream**: Messaging framework for microservices, enabling event-driven architectures.

6. **Spring Cloud Sleuth**: Provides distributed tracing to help monitor microservices communication.

# 2. Using Spring Cloud Config for Centralized Configuration Management

In a microservices architecture, managing configuration files for each service becomes increasingly difficult as the number of services grows. **Spring Cloud Config** provides a centralized way to manage configuration across all services.

## Why Use Spring Cloud Config?

1. **Centralized Management**: You only need to manage one configuration file, which can be shared by multiple microservices.

2. **Dynamic Configuration Updates**: Configurations can be updated without restarting your services.

3. **Environment-Specific Configuration**: You can easily have separate configurations for different environments (e.g., dev, prod).

4. **Version Control**: Spring Cloud Config can pull configuration files from version control systems such as **Git**, making it easy to track changes over time.

## Setting Up Spring Cloud Config

To integrate **Spring Cloud Config** into your application, follow these steps:

### Step 1: Set Up the Config Server

1. Create a Spring Boot project for the **Config Server**. Add the following dependencies in pom.xml:

```
<dependency>
    <groupId>org.springframework.cloud</groupId>
```

```
<artifactId>spring-cloud-starter-config</artifactId>
</dependency>
<dependency>
  <groupId>org.springframework.boot</groupId>
  <artifactId>spring-boot-starter-web</artifactId>
</dependency>
```

2. Create a **ConfigServer** application:

```
@EnableConfigServer
@SpringBootApplication
public class ConfigServerApplication {

  public static void main(String[] args) {
    SpringApplication.run(ConfigServerApplication.class, args);
  }
}
```

3. In application.yml, configure the **Config Server** to fetch properties from a **Git repository** or file system:

```
spring:
  cloud:
    config:
      server:
        git:
          uri: https://github.com/yourrepo/config-repo
```

### Step 2: Set Up Config Clients

Each microservice that needs configuration will become a **config client**:

1. Add the following dependencies to each microservice's pom.xml:

```
<dependency>
    <groupId>org.springframework.cloud</groupId>
    <artifactId>spring-cloud-starter-config</artifactId>
</dependency>
```

2. In application.yml of the microservices, point to the **Config Server**:

```
spring:
  application:
    name: task-service
  cloud:
    config:
      uri: http://localhost:8888  # URL of the Config Server
```

3. Now, you can define a configuration file, such as application-task-service.yml, in the **Config Server** repository.

---

# 3. Implementing Service Discovery with Eureka

### What is Service Discovery?

In a microservices architecture, services need to discover and communicate with each other. **Service Discovery** is a key component that helps microservices find and interact with other services in a dynamic environment.

**Spring Cloud Netflix Eureka** is a service discovery server that allows services to register themselves and discover others.

## Setting Up Eureka Server

1. **Create a Eureka Server**:

   o Create a Spring Boot project for the Eureka server and add the following dependencies:

```
<dependency>
    <groupId>org.springframework.cloud</groupId>
    <artifactId>spring-cloud-starter-netflix-eureka-server</artifactId>
</dependency>
<dependency>
    <groupId>org.springframework.boot</groupId>
    <artifactId>spring-boot-starter-web</artifactId>
</dependency>
```

2. Enable Eureka server by adding @EnableEurekaServer to your application:

```
@EnableEurekaServer
@SpringBootApplication
public class EurekaServerApplication {

    public static void main(String[] args) {
        SpringApplication.run(EurekaServerApplication.class, args);
    }
```

```
}
```

3.  In application.yml, configure the **Eureka Server**:

```yaml
spring:
  application:
    name: eureka-server
  cloud:
    netflix:
      eureka:
        client:
          registerWithEureka: false
        server:
          enableSelfPreservation: false
```

4.  Start the Eureka Server on port 8761.

---

## Setting Up Eureka Client

1.  Add **Eureka Client** to your microservice:

```xml
<dependency>
    <groupId>org.springframework.cloud</groupId>
    <artifactId>spring-cloud-starter-netflix-eureka-client</artifactId>
</dependency>
```

2.  In the application.yml of the microservice, register the service with Eureka:

```yaml
spring:
  application:
    name: task-service
```

```
cloud:
  netflix:
    eureka:
      client:
        serviceUrl:
          defaultZone: http://localhost:8761/eureka/
```

3. Use @EnableEurekaClient to enable service registration:

```
@SpringBootApplication
@EnableEurekaClient
public class TaskServiceApplication {

    public static void main(String[] args) {
        SpringApplication.run(TaskServiceApplication.class, args);
    }
}
```

---

# 4. Handling Fault Tolerance with Hystrix and Resilience Patterns

## What is Hystrix?

**Hystrix** is a library from **Netflix** that helps with **fault tolerance** and **resilience** in distributed systems. It implements the **Circuit Breaker** pattern, which prevents failures in one part of the system from cascading to other parts.

**Key Concepts of Hystrix:**

- **Circuit Breaker**: A mechanism that detects failures and prevents the system from trying to execute an operation that is likely to fail.

- **Fallbacks**: Provides fallback logic when a service fails.

- **Timeouts**: Ensures that requests that take too long are stopped before they can overload the system.

## Setting Up Hystrix in Spring Boot

1. Add the following dependency to the pom.xml of your service:

```
<dependency>
    <groupId>org.springframework.cloud</groupId>
    <artifactId>spring-cloud-starter-netflix-hystrix</artifactId>
</dependency>
```

2. Enable Hystrix in your application by adding @EnableHystrix:

```
@EnableHystrix
@SpringBootApplication
public class TaskServiceApplication {

    public static void main(String[] args) {
        SpringApplication.run(TaskServiceApplication.class, args);
    }
}
```

3. Use @HystrixCommand to define fallback logic:

```
@Service
```

```
public class TaskService {

    @HystrixCommand(fallbackMethod = "defaultTaskList")
    public List<Task> getAllTasks() {
        // Simulate a service call to another microservice
        return restTemplate.getForObject("http://user-
service/users/{id}/tasks", List.class, 1);
    }

    public List<Task> defaultTaskList() {
        return Collections.emptyList();  // Fallback response
    }
}
```

This ensures that if the **User Service** fails, the **Task Service** will return an empty list instead of failing.

---

# 5. Hands-On Project: Integrating Spring Cloud into Your Microservices Architecture for Service Discovery and Resilience

## Step 1: Set Up Eureka Server

1. Create a Spring Boot application for the **Eureka Server** and enable it with @EnableEurekaServer.

2. Configure it to run on port 8761.

### Step 2: Set Up Eureka Clients for Task and User Services

1. Modify your **Task Service** and **User Service** applications to register with Eureka.

2. Add the @EnableEurekaClient annotation and the Eureka configuration in the application.yml.

### Step 3: Set Up Hystrix for Fault Tolerance

1. Add **Hystrix** to the **Task Service**.

2. Use @HystrixCommand to define fallback methods for inter-service communication.

3. Test the fault tolerance by simulating failures in the **User Service**.

### Step 4: Test the System

1. Start all the services: **Eureka Server, Task Service**, and **User Service**.

2. Test the communication between the **Task Service** and **User Service** using Eureka.

3. Test fault tolerance by disabling the **User Service** and observing how **Task Service** handles the failure using the fallback method.

---

# Conclusion

In this chapter, we explored **Spring Cloud** and its powerful features for building scalable and resilient microservices. We learned how to manage centralized configuration with **Spring Cloud Config**, implement service discovery with **Eureka**, and ensure fault tolerance with **Hystrix**.

# Chapter 12: Containerizing Spring Boot Applications with Docker

## Overview

In this chapter, we will dive into the exciting world of **Docker** and explore how to containerize **Spring Boot applications**. Containerization has become a cornerstone of modern software development, allowing developers to package applications and their dependencies into standardized units (containers) that can be run on any machine with Docker installed.

We'll break down the **concept of Docker**, why containerization is essential for building modern applications, and walk you through the process of **creating Docker images** for your **Spring Boot** applications. We'll also cover **Docker Compose**, which allows us to manage multi-container applications and bring everything together in a practical, hands-on project.

By the end of this chapter, you'll have the skills to containerize your Spring Boot microservices and run them seamlessly inside Docker containers, making it easier to deploy, scale, and manage your applications.

---

### Key Topics Covered

1. **What is Docker and Why Containerization is Important**

2. **Creating Docker Images for Spring Boot Applications**

# 1. What is Docker and Why Containerization is Important

## What is Docker?

**Docker** is an open-source platform designed to automate the deployment, scaling, and management of applications inside **containers**. A container is a lightweight, standalone, and executable package that contains everything needed to run a piece of software, including the code, runtime, libraries, and system tools.

Containers provide a way to **package applications** and their dependencies into a **consistent environment** that can run anywhere—on a developer's laptop, in a testing environment, or in production.

**Key Features of Docker:**

1. **Lightweight**: Unlike virtual machines, containers share the host operating system's kernel and do not require a full OS. This makes them faster and more efficient.

2. **Portable**: Docker containers can run on any system that supports Docker, making them highly portable across different environments (local development, testing, staging, production).

3. **Isolation**: Containers isolate applications from each other and from the host system, ensuring that they don't interfere with one another.

4. **Consistency**: Docker ensures that the application runs the same way across all environments by bundling everything it needs inside the container.

## Why is Containerization Important?

1. **Consistency Across Environments**: Containerization eliminates the "it works on my machine" problem. Since containers include everything the application needs, the environment is guaranteed to be consistent across various stages of development and deployment.

2. **Simplified Deployment**: With Docker, you can deploy your application as a container without worrying about dependencies or conflicts with the host system.

3. **Scalability and Flexibility**: Docker makes it easy to deploy multiple instances of your application (scaling) and ensures that each instance is isolated from others.

4. **Microservices Architecture**: Docker fits perfectly into **microservices** architecture, where each service can run in its own container, simplifying deployment and scaling.

5. **Improved Developer Productivity**: Docker simplifies the process of setting up and configuring environments. Developers can focus on writing code instead of worrying about environment configuration.

# 2. Creating Docker Images for Spring Boot Applications

### What is a Docker Image?

A **Docker image** is a snapshot of a container. It contains the application and all of its dependencies, including the runtime, libraries, and configuration files. Once an image is created, it can be deployed to any system that supports Docker.

### Creating a Docker Image for a Spring Boot Application

Let's go step by step to create a **Docker image** for a **Spring Boot application**.

### Step 1: Set Up the Spring Boot Application

First, you'll need a basic Spring Boot application. If you don't have one yet, create a simple Spring Boot project using **Spring Initializr** (https://start.spring.io/) with the following dependencies:

- **Spring Web**

- **Spring Boot DevTools** (optional, for development)

Here's a simple TaskService in the TaskController:

```
@RestController
@RequestMapping("/tasks")
public class TaskController {

    private List<String> tasks = new ArrayList<>();

    @PostMapping
    public String addTask(@RequestBody String task) {
```

```
    tasks.add(task);
    return "Task added successfully!";
}


@GetMapping
public List<String> getAllTasks() {
    return tasks;
}
}
```

## Step 2: Add a Dockerfile

To build a Docker image for your Spring Boot application, you need a **Dockerfile**, which is a script that contains instructions for building the image.

Create a file named Dockerfile (without any extension) in the root directory of your Spring Boot project:

```
# Use the official OpenJDK base image
FROM openjdk:11-jre-slim


# Set the working directory inside the container
WORKDIR /app


# the JAR file from the local machine to the container
target/your-application.jar /app/application.jar


# Expose the port your application runs on (default Spring Boot
port is 8080)
```

*EXPOSE 8080*

*# Run the application*
*ENTRYPOINT ["java", "-jar", "application.jar"]*

### Step 3: Build the Docker Image

1. **Package the Spring Boot application** into a JAR file using Maven or Gradle.

If you are using Maven, run the following command in your terminal:

mvn clean package

This will generate the JAR file in the target directory.

2. **Build the Docker image:**

In the root directory of your project (where the Dockerfile is located), run the following command:

docker build -t spring-boot-app .

This will build the Docker image with the tag spring-boot-app.

3. **Verify the Docker image:**

Once the build is successful, you can list all Docker images with the command:

docker images

---

# 3. Running Spring Boot Applications Inside Docker Containers

Now that we have built the Docker image, let's run it inside a container.

### Step 1: Run the Docker Container

To run the application inside a container, use the following command:

docker run -p 8080:8080 spring-boot-app

This will run the Spring Boot application in a container, mapping port 8080 from the container to port 8080 on your local machine. You can now access the application by navigating to http://localhost:8080.

### Step 2: Verify the Application Is Running

Open your browser and go to http://localhost:8080/tasks. You should see a response indicating that the application is running.

You can also test the **POST** and **GET** endpoints using **Postman** or **curl**.

# 4. Docker Compose for Multi-Container Applications

In microservices, you often have multiple services running, each in its own container. **Docker Compose** is a tool that allows you to define and run multi-container Docker applications. With Docker Compose, you can manage and configure all of your containers in one place.

### What is Docker Compose?

**Docker Compose** is a tool that allows you to define multi-container applications using a **YAML file** (docker-compose.yml). It simplifies the process of running complex applications by managing dependencies and allowing you to start all containers at once.

# Setting Up Docker Compose for Multi-Container Microservices

Let's integrate Docker Compose into your Spring Boot microservices setup. Assume we have two services: **User Service** and **Task Service**, each running in its own container.

### Step 1: Create the docker-compose.yml File

In the root directory of your project, create a file named docker-compose.yml:

```
version: '3'
services:
  user-service:
    image: user-service-image
    build:
      context: ./user-service
    ports:
      - "8081:8081"
    environment:
      - SPRING_PROFILES_ACTIVE=prod

  task-service:
    image: task-service-image
    build:
      context: ./task-service
    ports:
      - "8080:8080"
    depends_on:
```

*- user-service*

**Explanation:**

- **version**: The version of Docker Compose we're using.

- **services**: Defines the different services (containers) we are using. In this case, **User Service** and **Task Service**.

- **build.context**: Specifies the directory where Docker can find the Dockerfile to build the image.

- **ports**: Maps the ports on the container to the ports on the host machine.

- **depends_on**: Ensures that the **Task Service** starts after the **User Service** is up.

---

## Step 2: Build and Run Multi-Container Application

To build and run all containers with Docker Compose:

1. Run the following command in the directory where docker-compose.yml is located:

2. docker-compose up --build

3. This will build the images for each service (if they haven't been built already), and then start all the services in their own containers. You can now access the **User Service** on port 8081 and the **Task Service** on port 8080.

---

# 5. Hands-On Project: Containerize Your Spring Boot Microservices and Run Them with Docker Compose

Let's implement a simple hands-on project where we containerize two Spring Boot microservices (**Task Management Service** and **User Management Service**) and manage them using **Docker Compose**.

### Step 1: Create Two Spring Boot Services

1. **User Management Service**: This service will handle user data (as shown earlier).

2. **Task Management Service**: This service will manage tasks and rely on the **User Management Service** for user data.

Both services will have their own Dockerfile, as shown in earlier sections.

### Step 2: Configure Docker Compose

Create the docker-compose.yml file as outlined above to manage both services.

### Step 3: Build and Run the Containers

1. Build and run the multi-container application using:

2. docker-compose up --build

3. Test the services by making API requests to both the **User Management** service (http://localhost:8081) and the **Task Management** service (http://localhost:8080).

# Conclusion

In this chapter, we covered the fundamentals of **Docker** and how it enables the **containerization of Spring Boot applications.** You learned how to build Docker images for your microservices, run those images inside containers, and manage multi-container applications with **Docker Compose.** By integrating Docker into your microservices architecture, you made your applications more portable, scalable, and easier to deploy.

# Chapter 13: Continuous Integration and Deployment with Jenkins and GitHub

## Overview

As applications grow and evolve, manually testing and deploying new versions becomes increasingly inefficient and error-prone. This is where **Continuous Integration (CI)** and **Continuous Deployment (CD)** come into play. These practices help automate the processes of testing, building, and deploying applications, making them faster, more reliable, and easier to maintain.

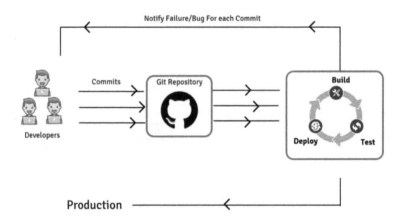

In this chapter, we will explore how to set up an **automated CI/CD pipeline** using **Jenkins** and **GitHub**. We will walk through the process of integrating **GitHub** with **Jenkins** to automatically trigger builds and deployments. Additionally, you will learn how to automate testing and deployment to staging and production environments, ensuring that your applications are always up-to-date and working as expected.

By the end of this chapter, you'll have a robust CI/CD pipeline in place that automates the testing, building, and deployment of your **Spring Boot** microservices applications.

---

## Key Topics Covered

1. **Introduction to Continuous Integration and Continuous Deployment**

2. **Setting Up a CI/CD Pipeline with Jenkins**

3. **Integrating GitHub with Jenkins for Automated Builds**

4. **Automating Tests and Deployments to Staging or Production Environments**

5. **Hands-On Project: Set Up Jenkins to Build and Deploy Your Microservices Applications Automatically**

---

# 1. Introduction to Continuous Integration and Continuous Deployment

### What is Continuous Integration (CI)?

**Continuous Integration (CI)** is a software development practice where developers frequently commit code changes to a shared repository. Each change is automatically built, tested, and integrated with the rest of the application. This practice aims to detect errors early, improve collaboration, and keep the software delivery pipeline smooth.

## Benefits of Continuous Integration:

- **Early Bug Detection**: Frequent integration of code ensures that bugs are detected early in the development cycle, making them easier to fix.

- **Automated Testing**: By running tests automatically with each commit, CI ensures that new changes don't break the existing functionality of the application.

- **Better Collaboration**: Developers can work in parallel on different features, and CI will automatically merge their changes without manual intervention.

## How Does Continuous Integration Work?

1. **Developers** commit their code changes to a shared version control system (like **GitHub**).

2. **Jenkins** or another CI tool detects the changes and starts a new **build** process.

3. **Automated tests** are run to ensure the changes don't break any existing functionality.

4. **Reports** are generated to provide feedback to the developers about whether the build was successful or if any tests failed.

## What is Continuous Deployment (CD)?

**Continuous Deployment (CD)** is an extension of **Continuous Integration**, where code changes that pass automated tests are automatically deployed to production. This reduces the time between writing code and making it available to users.

### Benefits of Continuous Deployment:

- **Faster Delivery**: New features, bug fixes, and improvements are delivered to users quickly.

- **Automated Deployment**: Deployments are done automatically, reducing the chances of human error.

- **Improved Reliability**: With automated deployment, there are fewer chances of failures during manual deployments, and the process is more repeatable.

### How Does Continuous Deployment Work?

1. **CI Tools** like Jenkins build and test the code after each commit.

2. Once the tests pass, the code is **automatically deployed** to a staging or production environment, depending on the configuration.

3. **Rollbacks** are possible if something goes wrong during the deployment, ensuring that production remains stable.

---

# 2. Setting Up a CI/CD Pipeline with Jenkins

### What is Jenkins?

**Jenkins** is an open-source automation server commonly used to implement **CI/CD pipelines**. It automates the process of building, testing, and deploying applications, allowing for continuous integration and continuous deployment.

Jenkins can:

- Automate builds for your Spring Boot applications.

- Run unit tests and integration tests.

- Deploy your applications to staging or production environments.

- Integrate with version control systems like **GitHub** to automatically trigger builds when code is pushed.

## Installing Jenkins

To set up a CI/CD pipeline, we first need to install **Jenkins.**

### Step 1: Download and Install Jenkins

1. **Install Java:** Jenkins requires Java to run. Install **Java 8** or higher.

To install Java:

```
sudo apt update
sudo apt install openjdk-11-jdk
```

2. **Install Jenkins:**

   o On **Ubuntu,** you can install Jenkins using the following commands:

```
wget -q -O - https://pkg.jenkins.io/jenkins.io.key | sudo apt-key add -
sudo sh -c 'echo deb http://pkg.jenkins.io/debian/ stable main >
/etc/apt/sources.list.d/jenkins.list'
sudo apt update
sudo apt install jenkins
```

After installing, start Jenkins:

```
sudo systemctl start jenkins
sudo systemctl enable jenkins
```

3. **Access Jenkins:** Open your browser and go to http://localhost:8080. You'll be asked for a **setup password,** which can be retrieved using:

4. sudo cat /var/lib/jenkins/secrets/initialAdminPassword

5. **Install Suggested Plugins**: Follow the on-screen instructions to install the recommended plugins and set up your Jenkins instance.

## Step 2: Setting Up Jenkins Jobs

Create a New Jenkins Job

Once Jenkins is up and running, the next step is to create a **new Jenkins job** that will handle the build process for your Spring Boot application.

1. **Open Jenkins** and click on **New Item**.

2. Select **Freestyle Project** and give your job a name (e.g., **SpringBoot-Project-Build**).

3. Under **Source Code Management**, choose **Git** and enter the URL of your GitHub repository.

   o Example:

   o https://github.com/yourusername/your-spring-boot-project.git

4. Under **Build Triggers**, select **GitHub hook trigger for GITScm polling**. This option ensures that Jenkins triggers a build whenever you push new code to GitHub.

5. Under **Build**, add the following shell command to build your Spring Boot application:

6. mvn clean install

7. Under **Post-build Actions,** you can choose to **archive the artifacts** (such as the JAR file) and **trigger downstream jobs** if needed.

---

# 3. Integrating GitHub with Jenkins for Automated Builds

## Step 1: Configuring GitHub Webhooks

To automatically trigger builds in Jenkins whenever code is pushed to your GitHub repository, you need to set up a webhook in **GitHub**.

1. **Go to your GitHub repository**.

2. Click on **Settings** > **Webhooks** > **Add webhook**.

3. Set the **Payload URL** to http://<your-jenkins-url>/github-webhook/.

4. Choose **Content type** as application/json.

5. Under **Which events would you like to trigger this webhook?**, select **Just the push event**.

6. Click **Add webhook**.

This webhook will now notify Jenkins whenever code is pushed to the repository, automatically triggering the build process.

## Step 2: Testing the Integration

1. Make a change in your code (e.g., update the README or modify a Java file).

2. Push the changes to GitHub.

3. Jenkins should automatically trigger the build process. You can monitor the progress by visiting Jenkins' **Build History**.

# 4. Automating Tests and Deployments to Staging or Production Environments

## Automating Tests

One of the primary goals of CI/CD is to run tests automatically with every build. This ensures that your application is always working as expected.

1. **Add Unit Tests to Your Project**: If you don't already have tests, you can add **JUnit** tests to your Spring Boot application.

Example of a simple test:

```
@SpringBootTest
public class TaskServiceTest {

    @Autowired
    private TaskService taskService;

    @Test
    public void testCreateTask() {
        Task task = new Task("Test Task");
        Task savedTask = taskService.createTask(task);
        assertNotNull(savedTask.getId());
    }
}
```

2. **Configure Jenkins to Run Tests**: In your Jenkins job, configure the **build** step to run **unit tests**. For a Spring Boot project, Jenkins will run the tests automatically as part of the mvn clean install command.

You can also configure Jenkins to show test results by adding the **JUnit plugin** and configuring it to collect test reports.

## Automating Deployments

Once the application is built and tested, the next step is to **automate deployments** to a staging or production environment.

1. **Deploy to a Staging Server**:

   o Use **Jenkins** to automatically deploy your application to a **staging server**. You can add a **Post-build Action** that uses a shell script or a deployment tool (such as **Ansible** or **Docker**).

Example script for deploying to a remote server:

scp target/your-application.jar user@staging-server:/path/to/deploy

ssh user@staging-server 'java -jar /path/to/deploy/your-application.jar'

2. **Deploy to Production**:

   o Similar to staging, you can set up **automated deployment to production**, ensuring that code changes are smoothly and safely deployed to the production environment.

# 5. Hands-On Project: Set Up Jenkins to Build and Deploy Your Microservices Applications Automatically

## Step 1: Set Up the Jenkins Pipeline

1. **Create a New Jenkins Pipeline Job**: Choose **Pipeline** instead of a Freestyle project.

2. **Define the Pipeline Script**: You can define the pipeline as code using a **Jenkinsfile**, which is a file stored in your project repository.

Example of a simple Jenkinsfile:

```
pipeline {
    agent any
    stages {
        stage('Build') {
            steps {
                script {
                    sh 'mvn clean install'
                }
            }
        }
        stage('Test') {
            steps {
                script {
                    sh 'mvn test'
                }
```

```
        }
      }
    stage('Deploy') {
      steps {
        script {
          sh 'scp target/your-application.jar user@staging-
server:/path/to/deploy'
          sh 'ssh user@staging-server "java -jar
/path/to/deploy/your-application.jar"'
        }
      }
    }
  }
}
```

3. **Commit the Jenkinsfile**: Push the **Jenkinsfile** to your repository.

4. **Set up GitHub Webhook**: As described earlier, ensure that every push to GitHub triggers the Jenkins pipeline.

## Step 2: Test the Pipeline

1. Push a change to your **GitHub repository**.

2. **Jenkins** should automatically trigger the build, run tests, and deploy the application.

3. Check the build logs in Jenkins to verify that everything was successful.

# Conclusion

In this chapter, we covered the essential practices of **Continuous Integration** and **Continuous Deployment (CI/CD)** using **Jenkins** and **GitHub**. You learned how to:

- Set up Jenkins to build and test your Spring Boot applications automatically.

- Integrate **GitHub** with Jenkins for seamless automated builds triggered by code changes.

- Automate tests and deployments to a staging or production environment, ensuring fast and reliable releases.

By implementing these practices, you've automated your development pipeline, making it more efficient and reducing the chances of human error in the build and deployment process. In the next chapter, we will explore **advanced monitoring** techniques to keep track of the health and performance of your microservices applications.

# Chapter 14: Testing Your Spring Boot Applications

## Overview

Testing is a crucial part of modern software development. It ensures that your application works as expected, minimizes the risk of bugs, and helps maintain a high level of code quality. **Spring Boot** provides powerful tools for both **unit testing** and **integration testing**, which are essential for ensuring that the application works correctly at every level.

In this chapter, we'll dive into testing your **Spring Boot** applications, starting with **unit testing** and then moving on to **integration testing**. We'll explore how to write tests with **JUnit**, use **Mockito** for mocking dependencies, test **RESTful endpoints** using **MockMvc**, and test entire services in an integrated environment.

By the end of this chapter, you'll have a solid understanding of how to write effective tests for your Spring Boot applications, ensuring your microservices are robust and reliable.

---

### Key Topics Covered

1. **Introduction to Testing with Spring Boot**

2. **Writing Unit Tests with JUnit and Mockito**

3. **Integration Testing with Spring Boot Test**

4. **Testing RESTful Endpoints Using MockMvc**

5. **Hands-On Project: Write Unit Tests for Your API Endpoints and Integration Tests for Your Microservices**

# 1. Introduction to Testing with Spring Boot

## Why is Testing Important?

Testing is essential for several reasons:

1. **Detect Bugs Early**: Testing ensures that your application behaves as expected. It helps identify bugs during development, before they reach production.

2. **Confidence in Refactoring**: Tests give you the confidence to make changes to your code without the fear of breaking existing functionality.

3. **Documentation**: Tests serve as documentation of your code. They explain how a piece of code is supposed to behave.

4. **Maintainability**: Well-written tests make it easier to maintain and extend your application over time.

There are different types of tests:

1. **Unit Tests**: These tests focus on testing individual components in isolation. They are typically fast and ensure that a single piece of functionality works as expected.

2. **Integration Tests**: These tests check how different components interact with each other. They are essential for ensuring that your services and APIs work in a real environment.

3. **End-to-End (E2E) Tests**: These tests cover the entire flow of your application, often including interactions with the database and external systems.

In this chapter, we will focus on **unit tests** and **integration tests** using **JUnit** and **Spring Boot's testing tools**.

---

## Testing Tools in Spring Boot

Spring Boot provides excellent support for testing through several key tools:

1. **JUnit**: The most widely used testing framework in Java for writing unit tests.

2. **Mockito**: A mocking framework used to mock dependencies in unit tests.

3. **Spring Test**: Provides testing support for Spring applications, including **@SpringBootTest** for integration testing.

4. **MockMvc**: A tool for testing Spring MVC applications by simulating HTTP requests to your controllers.

5. **TestRestTemplate**: A convenience class for testing RESTful services in Spring Boot.

---

# 2. Writing Unit Tests with JUnit and Mockito

### What are Unit Tests?

**Unit tests** are designed to test individual units of code, typically a single class or method, in isolation. The primary goal of unit testing is to ensure that each unit of your code functions correctly on its own.

### Setting Up JUnit for Testing

Spring Boot comes with **JUnit 5** integrated by default, so you don't need to add any dependencies for basic JUnit functionality. However, to mock dependencies, you'll also need **Mockito**.

To add **Mockito** support, include the following dependency in your pom.xml:

```
<dependency>
    <groupId>org.mockito</groupId>
    <artifactId>mockito-core</artifactId>
    <version>3.8.0</version>
    <scope>test</scope>
</dependency>
For JUnit 5 support:
<dependency>
    <groupId>org.springframework.boot</groupId>
    <artifactId>spring-boot-starter-test</artifactId>
    <scope>test</scope>
</dependency>
```

## Writing Unit Tests Using JUnit and Mockito
### Test a Service Layer Method

Let's create a simple **TaskService** with a method that fetches tasks from a repository.

```
@Service
public class TaskService {

    private final TaskRepository taskRepository;

    @Autowired
    public TaskService(TaskRepository taskRepository) {
```

```
        this.taskRepository = taskRepository;
    }


    public Task getTaskById(Long id) {
        return taskRepository.findById(id)
            .orElseThrow(() -> new TaskNotFoundException("Task
not found"));
    }
}
```

To write a unit test for this method, we will **mock the repository** using **Mockito** to simulate the database interaction.

```
@ExtendWith(SpringExtension.class)
@SpringBootTest
public class TaskServiceTest {

    @MockBean
    private TaskRepository taskRepository;

    @Autowired
    private TaskService taskService;

    @Test
    public void testGetTaskById() {
        // Arrange
        Task task = new Task(1L, "Test Task");
```

*Mockito.when(taskRepository.findById(1L)).thenReturn(Optional.o f(task));*

> *// Act*
>
> *Task result = taskService.getTaskById(1L);*
>
> *// Assert*
>
> *assertNotNull(result);*
>
> *assertEquals("Test Task", result.getDescription());*
>
> *}*

*}*

**Explanation:**

1. **@MockBean:** This annotation is used to mock the TaskRepository bean, allowing us to simulate database behavior in the unit test.

2. **Mockito.when():** We use this to simulate the findById() method of the repository to return a mocked Task object.

3. **Assert statements:** We check that the returned task is not null and its description matches the expected value.

## Mocking Dependencies with Mockito

Mockito is essential for unit testing when your class has dependencies (e.g., services or repositories). You can mock these dependencies to isolate the class being tested.

**Example of Mocking a Dependency:**

Suppose we have a TaskController that depends on TaskService. Here's how you can mock the TaskService in a test.

```
@WebMvcTest(TaskController.class)
public class TaskControllerTest {

    @MockBean
    private TaskService taskService;

    @Autowired
    private MockMvc mockMvc;

    @Test
    public void testGetTaskById() throws Exception {
        Task task = new Task(1L, "Test Task");
        Mockito.when(taskService.getTaskById(1L)).thenReturn(task);

        mockMvc.perform(get("/tasks/1"))
            .andExpect(status().isOk())
            .andExpect(jsonPath("$.description").value("Test Task"));
    }
}
```

**Explanation:**

- **@MockBean**: Mocking the TaskService bean, which is injected into the controller.

- **MockMvc**: Used for simulating HTTP requests and testing the controller's behavior.

---

# 3. Integration Testing with Spring Boot Test

## What is Integration Testing?

**Integration tests** evaluate how different components of the application interact with each other. Unlike unit tests, which focus on individual components, integration tests check the integration between different layers (e.g., service, repository, and database).

## Setting Up Integration Tests

Spring Boot provides the **@SpringBootTest** annotation, which is used for **integration testing**. This annotation starts up the whole application context, allowing us to test the interaction between various components.

### Example of Integration Test:

```
@SpringBootTest
public class TaskServiceIntegrationTest {

    @Autowired
    private TaskService taskService;

    @Autowired
    private TaskRepository taskRepository;

    @Test
    public void testCreateTask() {
```

```
    Task task = new Task("Test Task");
    Task savedTask = taskService.createTask(task);

    assertNotNull(savedTask.getId());
    assertEquals("Test Task", savedTask.getDescription());
}


@Test
public void testGetTaskById() {
    Task task = taskRepository.save(new Task("Another Task"));

    Task foundTask = taskService.getTaskById(task.getId());

    assertEquals("Another Task", foundTask.getDescription());
    }
}
```

**Explanation:**

1. **@SpringBootTest**: This annotation loads the full Spring application context for the test, including the database.

2. We test both the **service layer** and **repository layer**, verifying that the service correctly interacts with the database.

# 4. Testing RESTful Endpoints Using MockMvc

### What is MockMvc?

**MockMvc** is a powerful tool provided by Spring for testing **Spring MVC** controllers. It allows you to simulate HTTP requests and validate responses without actually starting a web server.

## Testing REST APIs with MockMvc

Suppose we want to test the **TaskController**. Here's how you can write tests for REST endpoints.

```
@WebMvcTest(TaskController.class)
public class TaskControllerTest {

    @MockBean
    private TaskService taskService;

    @Autowired
    private MockMvc mockMvc;

    @Test
    public void testGetTaskById() throws Exception {
        Task task = new Task(1L, "Test Task");
        Mockito.when(taskService.getTaskById(1L)).thenReturn(task);

        mockMvc.perform(get("/tasks/1"))
            .andExpect(status().isOk())
```

```
        .andExpect(jsonPath("$.description").value("Test Task"));
    }
}
```

**Explanation:**

- **@WebMvcTest**: Loads only the web layer of your application (the controller) for testing, making the test faster and more focused.

- **MockMvc**: Simulates an HTTP GET request and verifies the response.

---

# 5. Hands-On Project: Write Unit Tests for Your API Endpoints and Integration Tests for Your Microservices

### Step 1: Set Up the Project

- Create a **Task Service** with basic CRUD operations.

- Set up the **Task Controller** with RESTful endpoints.

### Step 2: Write Unit Tests for TaskService

1. Test the individual methods of **TaskService**.

2. Mock the repository using **Mockito** and test the behavior of createTask() and getTaskById().

### Step 3: Write Integration Tests for TaskService

1. Use **@SpringBootTest** to write integration tests that verify the behavior of the service and repository together.

2. Test that tasks are created and retrieved correctly from the database.

## Step 4: Write REST API Tests Using MockMvc

1. Use **MockMvc** to test the **TaskController** endpoints (GET /tasks/{id}, POST /tasks).

2. Verify the responses, status codes, and JSON structure.

---

**Conclusion**

In this chapter, we explored the crucial topic of **testing** in **Spring Boot applications**. We covered how to write **unit tests** using **JUnit** and **Mockito** to mock dependencies and test individual components. We also learned how to write **integration tests** with **@SpringBootTest** to ensure that the application works as expected when different components are integrated. Finally, we explored how to test **RESTful endpoints** using **MockMvc** to simulate HTTP requests and verify the responses.

By following the hands-on examples, you now have the tools to write robust tests for your Spring Boot applications, ensuring they are reliable, maintainable, and scalable. Testing is a critical part of the development lifecycle, and with the knowledge gained in this chapter, you can confidently write tests that ensure your application works as expected.

# Chapter 15: Deploying Spring Boot Applications to the Cloud

## Overview

In this chapter, we will cover the essential process of deploying your **Spring Boot microservices** to the **cloud**, enabling you to scale your applications efficiently for production. The cloud offers several advantages, including scalability, availability, and cost-efficiency, making it an ideal platform for deploying modern applications.

We will explore popular cloud platforms such as **AWS, Google Cloud**, and **Microsoft Azure** and look at how to set up cloud environments for Spring Boot applications. We will also dive into **Continuous Deployment** (CD) and **Kubernetes** for container orchestration, which are essential tools for automating deployments and managing large-scale applications.

By the end of this chapter, you will know how to deploy your **Spring Boot microservices** to the cloud and use **Kubernetes** for orchestration, ensuring that your applications are scalable, resilient, and production-ready.

---

Key Topics Covered

1. **Introduction to Cloud Platforms (AWS, Google Cloud, Azure)**

2. **Setting Up Cloud Environments for Spring Boot Applications**

3. **Continuous Deployment to Cloud Platforms**

4. **Using Kubernetes for Container Orchestration**

5. **Hands-On Project: Deploy Your Microservices to AWS or Another Cloud Platform and Use Kubernetes for Container Orchestration**

# 1. Introduction to Cloud Platforms (AWS, Google Cloud, Azure)

## What is Cloud Computing?

**Cloud computing** refers to the delivery of computing services such as storage, databases, servers, networking, software, and analytics over the internet. It allows businesses and developers to access IT resources on-demand, eliminating the need for physical hardware and providing greater flexibility and scalability.

There are three main types of cloud services:

1. **Infrastructure as a Service (IaaS)**: Provides virtualized computing resources over the internet, including virtual machines, storage, and networking. Examples: **AWS EC2, Google Compute Engine**.

2. **Platform as a Service (PaaS)**: Provides a platform and environment for developers to build, test, and deploy applications without managing the underlying infrastructure. Examples: **Google App Engine, AWS Elastic Beanstalk**.

3. **Software as a Service (SaaS)**: Delivers software applications over the internet, typically on a subscription basis. Examples: **Google Workspace, Salesforce**.

## Popular Cloud Platforms for Deploying Spring Boot Applications

1. **Amazon Web Services (AWS)**:

   - **EC2**: Virtual machines that can host applications, including Spring Boot.

   - **Elastic Beanstalk**: A PaaS offering that simplifies the deployment of Java applications, including Spring Boot.

   - **ECS**: AWS's container service for managing Docker containers, often used in microservice architectures.

   - **EKS**: Managed Kubernetes service to orchestrate containerized applications.

2. **Google Cloud**:

   - **Google Compute Engine**: Similar to EC2, it offers virtual machines for hosting Spring Boot applications.

   - **Google Kubernetes Engine (GKE)**: A managed Kubernetes service that simplifies container orchestration and scaling.

   - **App Engine**: A PaaS that automatically handles infrastructure management for Java applications, including Spring Boot.

3. **Microsoft Azure**:

   - **Azure Virtual Machines**: Similar to EC2, Azure provides virtual machines to run applications.

   - **Azure App Service**: A PaaS that simplifies the deployment and scaling of Spring Boot applications.

- o **Azure Kubernetes Service (AKS)**: A fully managed Kubernetes service for deploying containerized applications.

## Why Choose the Cloud?

1. **Scalability**: Cloud platforms provide on-demand scaling, enabling you to handle traffic spikes by adjusting resources as needed.

2. **Cost Efficiency**: Pay only for the resources you use, eliminating the need to maintain expensive infrastructure.

3. **Global Reach**: Cloud services are available across the globe, enabling your applications to serve users with low latency.

4. **Reliability**: Cloud providers offer built-in redundancies and high availability, ensuring your applications stay up and running even in the event of hardware failures.

# 2. Setting Up Cloud Environments for Spring Boot Applications

## Setting Up AWS Environment for Spring Boot

Let's walk through setting up an environment in **AWS** for deploying a Spring Boot application using **Elastic Beanstalk** and **EC2**.

### Step 1: Create an AWS Account

If you don't have an AWS account, visit AWS and create an account. Once your account is active, log in to the **AWS Management Console**.

### Step 2: Set Up Elastic Beanstalk for Spring Boot

Elastic Beanstalk is a fully managed service that allows you to deploy and scale Spring Boot applications quickly. Follow these steps to deploy your Spring Boot app on **Elastic Beanstalk:**

1. **Package Your Application**: In your Spring Boot project, run the following command to package your application as a JAR file:

2. mvn clean package

3. **Create an Elastic Beanstalk Environment:**

   o Go to the **Elastic Beanstalk** console in AWS.

   o Click on **Create New Application**.

   o Choose **Web Server Environment** and select **Java** as the platform.

   o Upload your packaged JAR file.

   o Configure any environment variables, such as database connections, if necessary.

4. **Deploy the Application:**

   o After configuring the environment, click **Create Environment**.

   o Elastic Beanstalk will automatically create an EC2 instance, set up load balancing, and deploy your Spring Boot application.

5. **Access the Application:**

   o After deployment, you can access your application using the public URL provided by Elastic Beanstalk.

**Step 3: Setting Up EC2 for Spring Boot**

For more control over your environment, you may want to use **EC2** instances instead of Elastic Beanstalk. Here's how you can set it up:

1. **Create an EC2 Instance**:

   o   Go to the **EC2 Console** and click **Launch Instance**.

   o   Choose an **Amazon Machine Image (AMI)**. For Spring Boot, use a basic **Amazon Linux 2** or **Ubuntu** instance.

   o   Select the instance type (e.g., t2.micro for small applications).

   o   Configure security groups to allow traffic on ports 8080 (for Spring Boot apps) and SSH (port 22).

2. **Connect to the EC2 Instance**: Use **SSH** to connect to your EC2 instance. For example:

3. ssh -i your-key.pem ec2-user@your-ec2-public-ip

4. **Install Java and Dependencies**: Install **Java 11** and **Maven** (if not already installed) on your EC2 instance:

5. sudo yum install java-11-openjdk-devel

6. sudo yum install maven

7. **Deploy Your Spring Boot Application**:

   o   Upload your Spring Boot JAR file to the EC2 instance using **SCP** or any other file transfer method.

   o   Run the application using:

8. java -jar your-application.jar

9. **Access the Application:** Open your browser and visit http://your-ec2-public-ip:8080 to see your Spring Boot application running.

---

# Setting Up Google Cloud Environment for Spring Boot

## Step 1: Create a Google Cloud Account

Sign up for a **Google Cloud** account and log in to the **Google Cloud Console**.

## Step 2: Set Up Google Kubernetes Engine (GKE)

1. **Create a GKE Cluster:**

   o In the **Google Cloud Console**, navigate to **Kubernetes Engine** and click **Create Cluster**.

   o Choose the cluster configuration, such as the number of nodes, machine type, and region.

2. **Install the Google Cloud SDK:** Install the **Google Cloud SDK** on your local machine to interact with the Google Cloud Console via the command line.

3. **Deploy Your Spring Boot Application:**

   o **Containerize** your Spring Boot app by creating a **Dockerfile** (as described in Chapter 12).

   o Build the Docker image and push it to **Google Container Registry** (GCR).

```
docker build -t gcr.io/your-project-id/your-app .
docker push gcr.io/your-project-id/your-app
```

4. **Create a Kubernetes Deployment**: Create a Kubernetes deployment configuration file (deployment.yaml) to define how your Spring Boot app should run in the cluster.

```
apiVersion: apps/v1
kind: Deployment
metadata:
  name: your-app-deployment
spec:
  replicas: 3
  selector:
    matchLabels:
      app: your-app
  template:
    metadata:
      labels:
        app: your-app
    spec:
      containers:
       - name: your-app
         image: gcr.io/your-project-id/your-app
         ports:
          - containerPort: 8080
```

5. **Deploy to Kubernetes**: Use the following command to deploy the application to your GKE cluster:

```
kubectl apply -f deployment.yaml
```

6. **Access the Application**: Set up a **LoadBalancer** to expose your application publicly:

```
kubectl expose deployment your-app-deployment --
type=LoadBalancer --port=80 --target-port=8080
```

You can now access the application using the external IP provided by Google Cloud.

---

# Setting Up Azure Environment for Spring Boot

## Step 1: Create an Azure Account

Sign up for an **Azure** account and log in to the **Azure Portal**.

## Step 2: Set Up Azure App Service

1. **Create an App Service**:

   o Go to the **App Services** section in Azure and click **Create**.

   o Choose **Java** as the runtime stack and configure other details like subscription, region, and resource group.

   o Upload your Spring Boot JAR file.

2. **Deploy the Application**: Azure provides a simple deployment pipeline via **Git, FTP**, or **Azure CLI**. You can push your application code directly to Azure App Service.

3. **Access the Application**: Once deployed, you can access your Spring Boot application via the **Azure App Service** URL.

---

# 3. Continuous Deployment to Cloud Platforms

## Automating Deployments with Jenkins and GitHub

Once your cloud environment is set up, you can automate the deployment process using **Jenkins** and **GitHub**. This setup will automatically deploy your application whenever code is pushed to the **GitHub repository**.

## Set Up Jenkins for Continuous Deployment:

1. **Create Jenkins Jobs** to build and deploy your Spring Boot applications.

2. **Integrate Jenkins with GitHub** using webhooks, triggering Jenkins builds whenever new code is pushed to GitHub.

3. **Automate Deployment to Cloud**: Use shell scripts in Jenkins to push your built application to AWS, GKE, or Azure.

---

# 4. Using Kubernetes for Container Orchestration

## What is Kubernetes?

**Kubernetes (K8s)** is an open-source platform that automates the deployment, scaling, and management of containerized applications. It helps manage large-scale microservices architectures, providing tools for container orchestration, scaling, and ensuring high availability.

**Key Features of Kubernetes:**

- **Automated Deployment**: Kubernetes automates the deployment of containerized applications.

- **Scaling:** Kubernetes can automatically scale your application up or down based on traffic or resource utilization.

- **High Availability:** It ensures that your application runs with minimal downtime by maintaining multiple replicas of services.

- **Self-healing:** If a container fails, Kubernetes automatically restarts or replaces it.

---

# 5. Hands-On Project: Deploy Your Microservices to AWS or Another Cloud Platform and Use Kubernetes for Container Orchestration

### Step 1: Containerize Your Microservices

1. **Create Dockerfiles** for your Spring Boot microservices.

2. **Build Docker Images** and push them to **AWS ECR, Google Container Registry,** or **Azure Container Registry.**

### Step 2: Deploy Microservices with Kubernetes

1. **Set Up Kubernetes Cluster** using **AWS EKS, Google GKE,** or **Azure AKS.**

2. **Create Kubernetes Deployment Configurations** for each of your microservices.

3. **Deploy to Kubernetes** using kubectl apply -f deployment.yaml.

### Step 3: Set Up Load Balancer

Use Kubernetes to expose your services with a **LoadBalancer** to ensure that your application can handle high traffic.

---

# Conclusion

In this chapter, you learned how to deploy your **Spring Boot microservices** to the cloud using popular cloud platforms like **AWS**, **Google Cloud**, and **Azure**. We explored how to set up cloud environments, automate deployments with **Jenkins**, and orchestrate containers using **Kubernetes**.

www.ingramcontent.com/pod-product-compliance
Lightning Source LLC
Chambersburg PA
CBHW070947050326
40689CB00014B/3381